There Are No Electrons:

Electronics for Earthlings

Kenn Amdahl

D0029686

Clearwater Publishing Company, Inc.
PO Box 778
Broomfield, Colorado
80038-0778

There Are No Electrons: Electronics for Earthlings
Copyright 1991 by Kenn Amdahl
ISBN 0-9627815-9-2

Printed in the United States of America
First printing January, 1991
Second printing September, 1991
Third printing October, 1992
Fourth printing September, 1994
Fifth printingFebruary, 1997
Sixth printing June, 1998
Seventh printing June, 2000
Eighth printing July, 2004
Ninth printing July, 2006

Published by:

Clearwater Publishing Company, Inc
P.O. Box 778
Broomfield, CO
80038-0778

(303) 436-1982
(917) 386-2769 (fax)
www.clearwaterpublishing.com
kenn@clearwaterpublishing.com
Electronic ordering (EDI) via Mountain Book Company, a member of Pubnet.org, SAN 631-922X
www.mountainbook.org

About This Book

After seeing the movie "Star Wars," Kenn Amdahl realized that his young sons suddenly knew everything about Wookies and the Force, effortlessly, without study. Their minds were alert and engaged by all the fun in the movie, and therefore receptive to learning anything. Yoda could have taught them chemistry. On the other hand, if Han Solo and Luke Skywalker were described in the style of some traditional text books, they would seem dull as Victorian pinochle players. Darth Vader would be as hard to remember as the fourth President of the United States, whoever that was.

Kenn wondered if one could write engaging books on dull subjects that would make learning as effortless as watching a movie. To test his idea, he wrote this book about electricity, careful to keep the pace lively and the reading easy, entertaining, and irreverent. One would have to say it worked rather well.

But the concept was new and therefore seemed risky to publishers. The book was rejected by 89 different publishers and agents before Kenn decided all of them were simply wrong. He formed Clearwater Publishing and released it himself. Since then, it has been in print continuously, sold well, and generated an army of fans around the world. You are about to become one of them. Besides teaching thousands of people about electricity, this book helped inspire all the books for dummies and idiots, as well as helping to light the path for small publishers everywhere. Today, small companies publish more than half the titles released each year.

You'll enjoy this book even if you have no special desire to learn about electricity, just as you can enjoy Star Wars without a desire to understand light swords. The learning is a bonus: You won't be able to prevent it.

This book has been typeset in a more efficient style than the earlier printings. Despite fewer pages, it contains the complete text of the original. Some old, minor mistakes and typos have been replaced with new typos and mistakes.

Acknowledgements

I hate acknowledgement pages. They 're always just too darn sweet for me. On the other hand, thanking is cheaper than paying. So, thank you, everyone who helped, especially the following:

My wife Cheryl was understanding and supportive beyond all reason. She is, and has always been, my biggest fan and most perceptive reader.

Joe Reid convinced me to be less creative with my spelling, grammar and punctuation. It cost him many hours, several beers, and a few gray hairs. There are, apparently, well-established traditions for the use of commas, hyphens, and the various parts of speech, which he knows and I don't. Jenni Hadden helped duplicate his efforts for this printing.

My son Scott was the first human to read the manuscript. He was kind and generous, but firm. His suggestions changed the book. My son Paul helped keep me within the accepted parameters of sanity. My son Joey provided artwork for the first printing cover.

My father Bernhard Amdahl and my uncle Vince Backlund convinced me to modify the Greenie Theory to accommodate certain regularly observed electrical phenomena.

Larry Shirkey, photographic genius, took the picture for the front cover. William Braxton Lee (the renowned storyteller) and Christy Moeller modeled. Merle Ware was our look-out man. Ken Chomic provided the subtitle "Electronics for Earthlings."

Alan Bernhard, Carla Black, Al French, Bob Ide, Tom and Twyla Hansen, Bonnie Meadows, Anne Rocheleau, Randy and Gregg Schumacher, Sports Ink, Bill Sanders, Steve Price, and many other friends contributed.

Special thanks to the folks who were willing to lie on or near the back cover. I will never be able to repay the karmic investment they made on my behalf. Ray Bradbury, Dave Barry, Clive Cussler, George Garrett and the others – they all had better things to do than read this and lend their names. Please buy their books.

I'd also like to thank, in advance, every person who does not sue me for using their name or likeness (real or imagined) herein without permission. All characters are fictitious. It's not *the* Clint Eastwood, for example, or *the* Woody Allen. That would be absurd. It turns out there is a guy named Eddy Current, and he's in electronics, and he read the book, although I'd never heard of him before. What are the odds of that? He didn't sue me; let Mr. Current show all of us the way. Obviously, it's not *the* Microsoft. We *love* Mr. Bill. Pay no attention to that Macintosh behind the curtain.

Thanks to Dan Poynter for writing *The Self Publishing Manual.* If you're tired of rejection slips, buy his book.

And I'd like to thank you. That's right, you there, holding this book, reading these words. I'm glad you're here. I hope you enjoy our time together. I certainly will.

Table of Contents

Introduction

Some people honestly believe they understand electricity, just as alchemists once thought they understood how to transform lead into gold. Don't despise or ridicule these poor souls. They should be tolerated and gently educated until they are ready to rejoin society.

No one really understands electricity.

But no one wants to admit it.

Once I realized that truth, it became easy to learn *about* electricity.

Whatever it is (the accepted theory changes every fifty years or so), the stuff has been observed and studied for several hundred years. We can predict its behavior, just as an ancient witch-doctor could predict an eclipse. And we can use it, as a cook uses yeast, even though he doesn't know or care what all those microscopic critters are doing in his dough. We can learn plenty about electricity, and we use it every day.

Yet some people prefer to stay ignorant of the workings of electricity, because of a fear similar to the common fear of automobile engines. We know there's a monster lurking under the hood (or in those wires...). We know that it feeds upon gasoline and magic (or that it dwells in nuclear power plants and lightning...) and if we disturb it, it will strand us at the worst possible time (or electrocute us). Perhaps if we ignore it, it will leave us alone.

I am here to tell you that electricity is a trained elephant. It is big and strong, yes. We avoid the tusks and try not to let it step on us, of course. But it is a friendly giant, with a very simple mind, and it always responds to the commands it knows. A child can lead it like a puppy.

Electricity has less than a dozen observable characteristics; we seldom are concerned with more than half of these. Electricity is comparable in complexity to a facial tissue. A facial tissue may have length,

1

width, thickness, weight, color, fragrance, texture, some number of plies or layers, strength, absorbency, a brand name and a price. Add to that the fact that it may be either mine or yours, or of unknown origin, and that it may be either new or used, fresh and smooth or mashed together after months in last winter's coat pocket, or that it may have gone through the washing machine a time or two, and you can see that a facial tissue is a lot more complicated than electricity.

There are six ways to produce electricity; you need to understand two of them.

Of the six ways to get useful work out of electricity, only three are important.

And most of our manipulation of electricity is accomplished with a dozen or fewer devices in various combinations.

That's it.

When you understand two dozen concepts you'll feel comfortable with electricity. I have eaten coleslaw that had more ingredients. Electricity is simple.

But this beautiful and powerful mystery is hardly ordinary or boring. If there is magic in the universe, the evidence must surely be electricity and life itself. Just as we know enough about life to perform crude biological parlor tricks (grow hybrid corn, treat a simple disease), so we are children in the sorcerer's work-room playing with electrical spells we don't really understand. We can no more explain the inner workings of the electrical phenomenon than we can breathe life into a crescent wrench. Yet we have seen its power, and the few tricks we can perform make us feel wise indeed.

Shall we study this wonder the same way we study geography or algebra (subjects that really *are* boring)?

No. Like any magical thing, it should be studied by flashlight, under the covers, late at night so mom and dad won't know. Keep this book hidden in your own secret place. As you learn the magic words, the potions, the hexes and spells, you will unlock a remarkable force from another dimension. Your fear will slowly change to an eerie curiosity. You will find yourself wanting to know more, no matter the price.

Finally, you will call out in the stillness of your darkened room, "Show yourself! I am not afraid!"

You will force yourself to sit still, but your hands will be trembling. You will hear a sound somewhere in the darkness. And when that awesome grinning genie finally swells into the room, with blood red eyes and flashes of lightning showing through his ghostly mass, then you will wonder at your own brave foolishness and ache to run to some bright and safe place... but it will be too late. He will lean low until you feel his hot ozone breath on your cheek. His voice will crackle and hum like a high voltage power line as he whispers in your ear:

"You have summoned me, master. What is your command?"

There will be no time to check your notes. You will hold your breath, fight down your terror, and make a wish.

Telling yourself, over and over again, that you don't believe in magic.

The Author

Eugene Amdahl is probably a genius. For years he designed computers for IBM, then he started Amdahl Corporation (which is now a multi-million-dollar-a-year super-computer company) and began working on even more complicated and wonderful electronic ideas. His name is always spoken reverently by electrically inclined people.

I've never met Eugene Amdahl, but somebody told me he's my father's third cousin, once or twice removed. Or something like that.

My father, Bernhard Amdahl, worked for the telephone company for years, solving difficult electronic problems, teaching classes, doing telephone company stuff. One of my uncles, Vincent Backlund, repairs televisions for a hobby. My uncle John Amdahl taught electronics for the Navy. My uncle Lowell Amdahl repaired computers for IBM. Many of my relatives have been deeply involved with electronics.

So, you see, I acquired my electronics expertise not in the traditional way, through education. I got mine genetically.

3

Unfortunately, I was unaware of this gift. I thought I was a guitarist. I became more convinced that electronics was not a part of my destiny when I tried to read books that claimed they would teach me the subject. Immediately I noticed an interesting phenomenon. After about three pages, my eyelids began to droop and I felt a tremendous urge to go mow the lawn.

I nearly killed that lawn trying to learn electronics, but I persisted. I read 18 pounds of beginning electronics books, stole information from friends and relatives, and performed countless boring and unsuccessful experiments. The one rule I learned is the one that says beginning books must be dull and they must be written by guys who forgot years ago how confusing the language and culture can be when you are a foreigner in the land of electronics.

This book may be the exception. I consider my lack of a Ph.D. in electrical engineering to be one of my soundest qualifications for writing it. If you are completely ignorant about electronics, I am the guy for you. I can speak to you as an equal.

The Creative Use of Jargon

Nearly every area of human activity, from sports to medicine, has its own specialized vocabulary, its own "little language." These words and phrases are the "jargon" of the activity. When you learn to play golf, you learn about hooks, slices, chip-shots, eagles and birdies. When cooking, you baste, saute, marinate, reserve liquids and clarify your onions. And, by the time you finish this book, you'll be swapping voltage jokes with electrical engineers, gossiping about push-pull amplifiers with the TV repairman, and saying words like "resistance," "capacitance," and "frequency modulation" confidently, as if you understood them. Remember that most education is based on the premise that speaking the language is more important than having something to say. Learning the vocabulary of a hobby is part of the fun.

More than that, it's powerful. Jargon is the weapon of choice at cocktail parties and among people who "take lunches" with each other.

The creation of jargon is the primary activity of educators, sportscasters, politicians and street-gangs. Jargon provides the clearest distinctions between generations. ("Isn't that groovy? Isn't it boss?"/ "I don't understand, Dad. I thought it was totally phat.") Our various jargons are the dialects of American culture, our class distinctions, and the uniforms of our jobs and interests. Without them we would all seem pretty much the same. Jargon is diversity and freedom and democracy. Eliminating jargon is the first step on the road to communism.

As a practical matter, jargon serves two rather wonderful purposes. First, it's a short-hand for the people who understand it. A sportscaster couldn't possibly describe the individual movements of twenty-two football players racing around the field. Because of the language of "football-talk," he doesn't have to. He says, "The quarterback goes to the shotgun, both receivers split wide to the left. Single set-back. Eighty runs a post pattern, clearing the zone. Number Seven reads the safety blitz, dumps it off to the tight end on a quick comeback up the middle. He's hit immediately, but he got about five on it. Second down." Who needs television when you've got a guy who can describe the action like that? It's poetry.

Unless, of course, you don't understand the vocabulary. Which brings up the other wonderful thing about jargon: It can be used to confuse and exclude people who are not members of the club. I call this "the Pig-Latin Principle." Remember the gleeful feeling you got as a child, talking to your buddies in gibberish that your sister couldn't understand? Well, that's the same feeling that lawyers get when they say "caveat emptor," or "corpus delicti," or "ipso-facto." You'll notice, however, that when they truly wish to communicate they talk like this: "You owe me eight-hundred dollars. Pay now." No jargon there.

Suppose you want to fool someone into believing that you understand something. No problem; use jargon:

"Daddy, why does the TV picture go goofy when I touch the screen with my magnet?"

"That's easy, son. The magnetic lines of force deflect the stream of electrons in the cathode ray tube, causing a distortion in the raster."

"Wow, you sure are smart, Daddy!"

"Thanks, son."

5

Perhaps eighty-five per cent of the task of learning electronics is simply remembering about two dozen neat words. And they are, indeed, wonderful words, masterpieces of jargon. Magnificent phrases like "inductive reactance" flow effortlessly from the lips of guys who can't cook hot dogs or find the flashing blue light in a K-Mart store. That's important to keep in mind. It doesn't take a lot of brains to learn a few words. Parakeets and myna birds do it all the time. You can, too. It's not work, it's just a game.

Say we want to build a radio using only items we can find around the house. First, of course, we give the project itself an important-sounding title, like "Electronics Survival Drill" or "Self-Sufficiency Experiment." (Incidentally, this is the same process that is used in writing grant proposals.) We might be able to build the Vacuum Tube Diode Rectifier out of a big bottle, like the kind that gourmet lemonade comes in. Of course, you wouldn't want to use some old used bottle would you? No sir, this is Science. You're just going to have to go out and buy a new bottle and empty it yourself.

Of course, we could build a battery out of many different things, but I really prefer the batteries I make out of the liquid from those big, juicy pickles with a lot of garlic you get in the refrigerated section of the grocery store. Sure they cost a little more, but then you want to be careful around electricity. Cut corners when you're studying geography or Latin. Then we're going to need some resistors. Haven't you ever wondered how much resistance was in a half-pound roast beef sandwich? Me too. How about paper to use as the dielectric in your capacitors? I have found that the paper they use in a particular fishing magazine works especially well. For an antenna, I bet the aluminum tubing in one of those folding patio lounge chairs would be perfect. Or a long fishing pole might work. A True Scientist and Earnest Student would have both available and experiment to see which one works best.

I'm sure you are beginning to get the hang of it. I often sacrifice my weekends to the pursuit of scientific knowledge. My wife is understanding and supportive when I explain how I have to buy materials to make a vacuum tube diode, some capacitors, resistors and a battery. She gives me the money. Then, when I say that I want to conduct comparative antenna experiments somewhere far from all the electro-magnetic interference of the city, she makes me drive all the way out to Giant Trout Lake. I protest, of course, but finally my sense of responsibility wins out. After all, I have a strong commitment to education. I drive out to the lake with my lounge chair, fishing pole and other electrical components, and spend the weekend studying.

And that's the way we use jargon.

Static Electricity: A Cat's Nightmare

When you rub your shoes on the carpet and then touch your unsuspecting cat's nose, you are experimenting with static electricity. The satisfying little snap and the quick flash of light that proves to the world that you are not a "cat person" is not, technically speaking, static electricity, however. Static means un-moving, or stationary, and something zapped from your finger to the cat, obviously in motion. An electrical engineer would refer to it as a "spark." This is probably as good a time as any for us to begin learning technical terms like that. Whatever it is, if electricity isn't moving, we call it static electricity. A spark is electricity moving through air. Static electricity can cause sparks, but once it's moving, it's not static any more.

Static electricity is what filled your body when you shuffled your feet on the carpet. As you stood there grinning, saying, "Here kitty-kitty…" in your sweetest voice, you were loaded with the stuff. Except that your hair tended to stick out, you couldn't feel it, or smell it, or sense it in any way. The friction of your feet gathered something from the carpet, something invisible to all of your senses. Whatever it is, it can't be observed directly. The only evidence of its existence is the effect it has on things that we can observe. Things like cats, and sleeping grandparents.

In a similar way, droplets of water in a windy cloud gather static electricity through friction with the air. The billions of droplets in a single cloud can gather an awful lot of static electricity. The sparks formed this way are called lightning. Thunder heads are often brim-

7

ming with incredible amounts of static electricity as they cruise the suburbs in search of die-hard golfers.

The study of electricity began in ancient Greece when shepherds discovered that they could gather static electricity by petting their sheep with pieces of amber (petrified tree sap). It is hard to imagine why that first shepherd decided to try the experiment. It is also hard to imagine why they continued the practice long enough to make it into the history books, since there isn't a lot you can do with static electricity. I suppose it's evidence that they also had cats.

These unwashed illiterate sheep herders, camping for months with their flocks, rubbing the ones they could catch with amber, are the fathers of modern electronics. They discovered that the piece of amber became temporarily changed by this rubbing, and would now attract little bits of dried leaves, just like a magnet attracts iron. Wonderful trick though that is, the Greeks did not spend a lot of time developing it, and electricity remained a harmless novelty for about 18 centuries. Interestingly enough, the Greek word for amber is "electron."

During the 18th century (1700-1799) guys in tight pants and powdered wigs performed what were known as parlor tricks. After dinner, they would retire to the living room, (known back then as the parlor) and amuse the young ladies with gadgets and magic tricks involving things like magnets, mirrors and primitive household chemistry. This era is fondly referred to as "the Age of Enlightenment" and these parlor tricks evolved into what is now known as science. Because of one parlor trick, these fellows figured out that there are two different kinds of static electricity.

Our dapper heroes took a bar of hard rubber and rubbed it on some wool. This was called charging it.

A small, lightweight ball, made of the spongy material found inside dead weeds (pith) was suspended from a string.

Now, if they held the rubber bar close to the hanging pith ball, the ball would swing toward it. The charged rubber bar attracted the pith ball. However, if they let the two actually touch each other, after clinging together for a second or two, the ball would swing away from the bar. No longer attracted, it was actually repelled by the bar. By touching it, the bar had transferred some of its charge to the ball.

The experiment worked just as well if they charged a glass rod by rubbing it on silk. It would attract the pith ball for a long time, unless the two actually touched each other. If they touched, they would cling together for a minute, and then the ball would swing away from the rod and do its best to avoid the rod however it was chased.

Here's the interesting part: A pith ball that has been in contact with a charged rubber bar, while now repelled by that rubber bar (or any other charged rubber bar) is still attracted to a charged glass rod. And a pith ball charged by contact with a glass rod, will try to swing away from any charged glass rod, but will be attracted to a charged rubber bar. Kind of like some innocent puppy that chases both skunks and porcupines. If it catches a skunk, it learns its lesson and runs away from all future skunks, but it still chases porcupines.

Obviously, there are two kinds of static electricity. There's the kind you get by charging bars of hard rubber and the kind you get by rubbing glass and silk together. This parlor trick, and this deduction, are important only because all the rest of the science of electricity is based upon them. Otherwise I wouldn't even mention it. They could have named the two kinds of charge "Glass-Type Charge" and "Rubber-Type Charge." They could have named them "Bartholomew" and "Alfred." As it turns out, they named them "positive" and "negative."

By repeating the old pith ball trick dozens of times for the bored young ladies of the day, these fellows came to be pretty good at it and could predict what was going to happen. Each and every time, a charged object would attract an uncharged ("neutral") object. And two objects, one charged with positive static electricity and the other with negative, would be attracted to each other.

But two objects, both charged with positive static electricity, would repel each other. Two objects, both charged with negative static electricity, would also repel each other.

There have been many complicated theories over the years to explain why this is so. Most people are happy with the current explanation, a few aren't so sure. The experiment itself can be performed in dozens of variations by a child, and the results are consistent. Something magical happens when things are occupied by static electricity, and we remember it by the simple slogan:

"Like charges repel each other. Opposites attract."

A Brief Digression

It occurs to me that the world would be different, in subtle ways, if they had actually named the two types of charges Bartholomew and Alfred.

When we jump-start a car, we'd have to remember to connect Bartholomew to Bartholomew and Alfred to Alfred. We'd have to remember that electricity always flows from Alfred to Bartholomew and never from Bartholomew to Alfred.

A transistor has three sections; We'd have to label the two types of transistors as either Bartholomew-Alfred-Bartholomew transistors or Alfred-Bartholomew-Alfred transistors. Parts would have to be made larger to accommodate printing the names, and therefore heavier. With these larger, heavier parts, space flight would probably have been impossible.

In some ways, on the other hand, we would have been better off with Alfred and Bartholomew. The words "positive" and "negative" have caused us many problems. Back in the pith ball days, no one knew for sure if electricity moved, or if it was alive, or what. Ben Franklin was pretty sure it moved, only it moved so darned fast he couldn't tell which direction. In trying to organize the thinking about this infant science, he took a calculated mental gamble and suggested that it always moved in one direction, from one type of charge to the other. So far, he was correct. Pushing his luck, he guessed that it always moved from things with a positive charge toward things with a negative charge. After all the parlor experiments, those terms were established. This time old Ben bet on the wrong horse, however. Much later, with more modern instruments, we learned that electricity always moves from things that have a negative charge and toward things that have a positive charge.

This was embarrassing. Everyone loves Ben Franklin. After all, wasn't he the man who invented Daylight Savings Time as a joke, never thinking for a minute anyone would actually try the silly thing? Wasn't he a founder of our country? Now our scientists would have to say he was dead wrong. Worse than that, years and years had gone by, with textbooks written, devices invented and patented, final exams prepared and graded, all based on diagrams that had arrows pointing the wrong direction.

We had to change the textbooks, of course. We had to set the record straight. But, to be polite to old Ben, we created some jargon to make him look a little less foolish. The truth is that electricity always moves from negatively charged things toward positively charged things. But, if you're looking at an old diagram with arrows going backward, you don't say it's written wrong. You say that it is written in "conventional current." In conventional current, electricity goes from positive to negative, like Ben thought it did. "Conventional" is a great electrical jargon word which means "backward from what's really going on."

So now you've got two important things to remember. In static electricity, things with the same kind of charge ("like charges") will repel each other, while things with opposite charges (a positive and a negative) will attract each other. And when electricity, whatever it is, moves, it always moves from negative things toward positive things.

It would be a good rule for all of us to follow in our lives.

The Electron Theory:
Scientific Models and Watermelons

Man thinks in analogies, in fables, in parables. That is, he compares things he doesn't understand to things he does ("It's like bees pollinating flowers, son.") This makes facts understandable and easy to remember. We take subtle, confusing or complicated phenomena and translate them into simple little picture stories. ("The universe is like a watermelon, and the stars are its seeds.")

These "scientific models" are useful teaching tools and handy communications aids, but they are also dangerous, because no model is perfect. When we use an analogy or model too much, we risk losing sight of the reality the model tries to represent. In the worst case, we teach school children that our model itself is reality. Scientific thought has always been limited by the imperfections of its various analogies.

In most ways, electricity is not much like the models used to describe it. "It's like water flowing through a pipe;" "Radio waves are like ocean waves;" "Resistance is like friction." Although each of these may help you understand some aspect of electricity, you have to be constantly aware that they are all just little picture-stories, little teaching tools, and nothing else. It's not like bees pollinating flowers, really, son. It's better than that.

The electron theory is nothing more than one more rather elaborate scientific model which may or may not be perfectly accurate. Your teachers will tell you it is perfect, that it is truth. Then, next year, when it must be modified a bit to accommodate some new information, they'll tell you once again that it's perfect, it's truth, it's reality. It won't occur to them to apologize for lying to you last year.

On the other hand, humans do think in analogies. The electron theory, bizarre and outlandish as it seems to me, works for most people. Models should not be thrown out with the bath water. They are not dangerous as long as you remember Amdahl's First Law:

"Don't mistake your watermelon for the universe."

The Electron Theory: The Easter Bunny of Science

For a long time, static electricity was the only show in town. In the early 1800's, if you said you were an electrical engineer, that pretty much meant you liked to zap cat noses. Many more parlor tricks were devised, most of them based on the same attraction-repulsion concept. In order to create even neater tricks, people wanted to understand what was actually going on inside that pith ball.

Why does friction create static electricity?

Why do objects charged with static electricity attract things like pith balls and paper?

Why do opposite charges attract each other, and like charges repel each other?

The truth is, nobody knows for sure. In the last couple hundred years several theories have become popular, then faded and been replaced. Each one, in its time, was taught as truth. People have devised some marvelous parlor tricks (television, satellite communications and computers spring to mind) despite these changing theories. Ben Franklin, Thomas Edison and Albert Einstein each made contributions, even though they subscribed to different theories.

As I write this, the vast majority of people believe that the electron theory is truth. When I say "the vast majority" I mean "every single person who thinks about electricity except me." Given the history of man's theories, that doesn't bother me. In 1450 they called you a goofball and you flunked geography class if you didn't believe the world was flat. In 1900 you flunked physics if your calculations indicated it was possible for man to fly in machines. In 1980 you'd lose your tenure for suggesting that superconductors were possible at temperatures as warm as liquid nitrogen, though now we know they are. Today science teachers will think you're more than just a bit odd if you don't believe in the electron theory. They certainly won't accept you into graduate school, let alone allow you to repair their TV set.

Therefore, you need to know enough about the electron theory to pass for one of Them – should you ever get surrounded by a mob of high school science teachers, for example. Your life may depend on it. If you find some irritating inconsistencies in the electron theory, don't worry. That only means that your brain is still alive. Just remember, it's called a theory because it has never been proven. True believers will insist that anyone with a pure heart will accept it on faith, this collection of bizarre, supposedly self-evident truths. Of course, that's also what they said during the Spanish Inquisition, and the Salem witch trials.

The electron theory maintains that everything in the universe is made of tiny particles called molecules, most of which are too small to be distinguished even when using the best microscopes in the world.

You will know you're dealing with a molecule, and not something larger, this way: If you try to break it into smaller pieces you'll change the nature of the material. For example, if you took a single molecule of salt, and broke off even a little of it, it would no longer be salt. It wouldn't taste like salt or act like salt. Some of it would look and act like sodium, while some of it would look and act like chlorine. Chlorine is a poisonous gas, by the way, so if you decide to split up some salt molecules, don't sprinkle any on your tomato sandwich. The smallest amount of salt you can have is one molecule.

But molecules are not the smallest critters in the zoo. Salt molecules are built out of sodium molecules and chlorine molecules. Water molecules are built out of hydrogen molecules and oxygen molecules. These, again, can't be broken down any further without changing the nature of the stuff. Chip away at a hydrogen molecule and you get something that is no longer hydrogen. At one point in history, someone decided that the substances that couldn't be broken down at all (by the methods available to them) were the smallest, simplest things that could be known. They were the building blocks, or elements, of every other substance. Scientists made a systematic list of these elements and started writing chemistry books.

Then someone figured out that elements must be made of even smaller parts. It was the only way to explain the results of their experiments. Different models were tried. The one that stuck says that molecules are built out of atoms.

Atoms are visualized as tiny solar systems. They have a massive central part, called a "nucleus," with little bitty satellites called "electrons" spinning around them. These electrons are so tiny that some early books said they have no weight.

The nucleus is made of relatively large and heavy components. There are two types of items that might be found in a nucleus. One kind is a proton, which always has a positive charge. Picture a proton as a big yellow pumpkin. A nucleus always has at least one proton. It may have several clustered together, like a mass of pumpkins glued together into a big ball. A nucleus may also have one or more neutrons. Picture a neutron as a big green watermelon. Neutrons are just as massive as protons, but they have no charge.

So, you have a mass of pumpkins and watermelons glued together into a bulky decoration to hang in your living room. Since protons always have a positive charge, and neutrons have no charge at all, the whole affair has a positive charge. The more protons, the more charge. Adding neutrons (watermelons) increases the weight of the nucleus, but doesn't affect the charge.

Picture the electrons that are buzzing around this huge vegetable sculpture as mosquitoes. Each mosquito (electron) has a negative charge. In fact, each one has exactly the same amount of negative charge as one pumpkin (proton) has positive charge. Since opposites attract, each pumpkin will attract exactly one mosquito. If there are five pumpkins hanging there, there will probably be five mosquitoes in frenzied orbit. Those nasty little bugs are moving so fast that even in our model we can't see them. All we see is a blurry haze, like a cloud surrounding the nucleus.

The electrons organize themselves around the nucleus in very specific flight patterns. According to the theory, they form layers around the nucleus, like the layers in an onion. Each layer can accommodate only a certain number of electrons. When the layer closest to the nucleus is filled, the next layer starts filling up, and so on. The electrons in the layers closest to the nucleus feel its attraction the most, and are the most difficult to disturb. They paid a lot of money to get front-row seats, and they don't care if it rains. They're going to stay.

Electrons that can't be disturbed easily are called "bound" electrons.

The outermost layer or "level" of electrons is the most interesting. In the atoms of some materials, the electrons in the outer layer are held relatively loosely. It doesn't take much effort to dislodge them. These are called "free" electrons. Once an electron is knocked away from the atom, it goes bouncing around through the material and will probably knock other electrons loose.

The electron theory, in a nutshell, says that electricity is this movement of free electrons. Static electricity occurs when there is not an equal number of protons (with their positive charges) and electrons (with their negative charges). The nucleus is massive, like the pumpkin and watermelon decoration which you have forgotten to remove from your living room. The electrons, like mosquitoes, are highly mobile. So, if anything is going to move, it's going to be the electrons. Electrons are repelled by other electrons. (All electrons have a negative charge. Like charges...) Electrons are attracted to positive charges (opposites...) An atom which for some reason has more protons than electrons will have positive charges which are not off-set by negative charges. It will have vacancies in its outer shell. Electrons will be attracted to it.

How does the electron theory explain the pith ball trick? When we shuffle our feet on the carpet, it says, we somehow accumulate extra electrons in our body. Our body is, therefore, negatively charged. These electrons tend to repel each other. They move as far away from each other as they can, and wind up being concentrated on our skin. The electrons on the skin of our finger repel electrons in the pith ball. Electrons flee from its charge. Pretty soon we have chased enough electrons away from our finger that they are concentrated on the far side of the ball. That means that the near side has too many protons; it has a positive charge. The negative charge on our finger, and the positive charge on the near side of the ball will attract each other. One of two things will happen. The electrons will leap across the gap, and we will see a spark. Or the protons, locked together in the pith ball, will move as a group toward our finger. They will pull the rest of the ball with them.

If we touch the ball, electrons stream from our body onto the ball until it has many more than usual. It has as many as it can hold. We have given it a negative charge. Now the ball is repelled by our still-negative finger.

It's a slick explanation. Oh, sure, it doesn't answer the questions: Why do like charges repel each other? Why do opposites attract? What does a proton have that an electron wants? And what is a charge, anyway? How did protons and electrons get them? And why don't neutrons have any? If you get more deeply curious, you will find people willing to tell you that an electron has no weight, yet it is subject to centrifugal force. But your science teacher says only things with weight are subject to centrifugal force. A few people will suggest that it does have weight yet it moves at speeds approaching the speed of light. Einstein proclaimed that to be illegal. Why are some electrons happily bound, while others with the same background are free?

The electron theory doesn't answer these questions. Your science teacher will say, who cares? And who cares that electrons have never been directly observed? We have seen streaks of light in cloud chambers that we think are the footprints of electrons. We have seen dots on photographic film that we believe were caused by electrons. True, we set up those experiments believing ahead of time that we would see evidence to support the electron theory, but that shouldn't matter, should it? It is widely accepted as truth. It works. That's why it's not called the electron hypothesis. On the other hand, it has never been conclusively proven. That's why it's not called the Electron Law.

Books have been written on the electron theory, courses have been taught, degrees granted. If you want to pass this course, (you will hear) stop making trouble.

Now comes the hard part. You must learn to smile and agree with them. Don't confront them, not yet. We are dangerously outnumbered. Imagine yourself transported in time back to old Salem, where they burned people suspected of conspiring with the Devil. Now imagine that it's bonfire season, and you realize you have somehow brought a television set and DVD player with you. Do you invite the neighbors in to watch your collection of Star Trek re-runs?

Another example: Imagine yourself as a single Oklahoma Sooners fan in Lincoln, Nebraska, in the wrong bleachers at the annual Football Game and Bone Crunching Ceremony. The biggest game of the year, the Grudge Match, The Hate Bowl. You are surrounded by 50,000 fans, all dressed in red, foam dribbling from their rabid lips, hate and anger in their eyes. Whose fight song are you going to sing?

"Of course there are electrons! I believe! I believe!"

Shout it out loud a few times. Then pull the covers back up over your head, turn on your flashlight and continue reading. There are no electrons. It's not like that at all.

The Ultimate Rubber Band Gun

Wait a minute, I hear you saying. Let me get this straight. Things that have the same charge repel each other, push each other away. Yet protons, those massive particles which have a positive charge, cluster together with each other and with neutrons to form the nucleus of atoms. Why don't they repel each other? What holds them together?

The answer is that they are held together by rubber bands. The protons want to repel each other. They push at each other just as hard as they can, but those little rubber bands are tough. They rarely break.

Of course, when they do break, the nucleus explodes. Protons and neutrons fly in every direction, releasing all their stored-up energy. Some of the energy escapes as heat, some as light, some as other forms of radiation. We're talking about a lot of energy here. If the movement of mosquito-electrons can do lightning-sized damage, imagine what happens when you start throwing pumpkins and watermelons around.

When one of those protons or neutrons, careening free like a crazy bowling ball, happens to slam into another nucleus, it's likely to break that nucleus' rubber bands, too. More protons and neutrons will be freed. This is called a "chain-reaction." If there are enough protons and neutrons bouncing around, the reaction will be self-sustaining. The material is radioactive. You might be able to see it glow.

If the material is dense, that is, there are many massive nuclei close to each other, and you've got enough chain reactions, a lot of heat, light and other radiation will be produced. The limiting factor becomes the physical size of your chunk of radioactive stuff. If it's small, the whole process is controlled; a lot of those wild and free nuclear particles won't run into another nucleus before they escape into the air. The heat produced in this situation can be captured and used.

If your chunk of radioactive stuff is bigger, the odds increase that each proton will bang into another nucleus before it flies free. More chain reactions will be started than are fizzling out. This point is called the "critical mass." When you exceed the critical mass, your atomic bomb explodes.

Scientists who try to picture everything as some variety of wave or field or force call the rubber bands "the strong force." Scientists who try to picture everything as some sort of particle call the rubber bands "gluons." This is because they glue the nucleus together. No one knows what really holds protons together in a nucleus. No one knows if there really are protons. They certainly don't know if there are electrons. But they know that if you break your rubber bands, you will blow a huge piece of real estate to smithereens.

You don't need to know any of this to study electricity. I just thought it was interesting.

A New Age Dawns:
Who's Moving Around Inside That Wire?

It's Little Greenies.

That's right. Little Greenies. It's not electrons at all. Electrons are a myth, a superstition. They don't make sense, they're boring, and they've never been proved. Shoot, I've never seen an electron, have you? Of course not. No one has. Sure, the electron theory seems to work a lot of the time, but so did the Flat Earth Theory. The theories of Aristotle, Newton and Euclid appeared to work pretty well, too, for a few hundred years. Now they seem childish. All because bold and adventurous thinkers like you and me were willing to consider alternatives.

Elegant and innovative alternatives, like The Greenie Theory.

I developed The Greenie Theory while fishing at a lake in Utah. It was one of those rare and special times when you have a whole city's water supply all to yourself. One of those days when the fish won't bite, but the sun is hot, the water is cool and clear, and you don't care. Cynics will try to convince you that the beer I was drinking provided most of my inspiration. I'm sure they said that about Einstein, too.

Anyway, as I started to work on that second six-pack, I experienced a vision, a revelation. Electricity suddenly made sense. All I had to do was forget the nonsense I had been trying to understand about charges and protons and neutrons, examine the evidence with an open

19

mind, and it became obvious. There were little guys inside those wires. Little green guys. Once I had that much, the rest fell into place. By the end of the day, not only had I filled in the details of The Theory, but I had proof positive that it was truth.

Like electrons, Little Greenies are too small to be seen. Even if you had a microscope that was infinitely powerful, you couldn't see them, because they're invisible. And, even if you had a tool that allowed you to see invisible things, you'd probably never corner one to study, because they're imaginary.

That may be the key to my whole theory, and why it will ultimately replace the electron theory. A big flaw of the electron theory is that scientists give electrons a whole truckload of outrageous characteristics and then ask us to believe that the little rascals are real. That is confusing. Real things can usually be proven. Real things don't have contradictory characteristics. Real things can be visualized. Scientists will tell you for example, that no matter how sophisticated our instruments get, it will always be impossible to know exactly where any one electron is at any certain time. It's part of the theory. Does that sound like a real thing?

On the other hand, people don't have any difficulty in accepting and believing in imaginary things (like a balanced federal budget, or UFOs, or lucky fishing shoes. Even now I hear you say, "Wait a minute! That's not fair! Those shoes really are lucky!") As long as we understand that something is imaginary, we don't have to justify it. We simply don't walk under the ladder, or sleep on the 13th floor. I bet the electron theory guys wish they had thought of it first. This little twist makes the Greenie Theory a near-perfect scientific model. It works in every case, it's easy to believe, and it's impossible to disprove. It would be like trying to disprove the existence of Santa Claus. Maybe you can't prove he exists, but it's even tougher to prove that he doesn't. And, as long as you believe, it doesn't really matter, does it?

But, as I said before, I have proof. I was working out some of the finer details of the theory, fishing pole in one hand, beer can in the other, sunburn spreading across my neck and shoulders, when I realized I wasn't alone.

"Psst!" The sound startled me and I dropped my fishing pole. It clattered on the rocky ground as I tightened my grip around the beer can in my other hand. At first I thought it was a snake, then I realized someone was trying to get my attention. Yet I knew I was the only human within 50 miles. I would have seen the dust if someone had driven up to the lake, and no one could have hiked in. Hesitantly I stood up and peered around the boulders. Someone was talking to me.

"Like, man, it's a bummer, can you dig it? Like, my foot, see, it's stuck in these rocks. Not cool, man, not in the program. Do you read me?"

It was a young man, very thin, in an a white T-shirt and cut-off jeans. His hair was light brown and hung down to his shoulders. He wore a red head-band. His features were pleasant enough, in fact, he would probably have been considered good-looking on a college campus, except for one slight irregularity. From his face to his bare feet, his skin was as green as spinach.

"What?" I said. The surprise of seeing anyone, let alone someone who looked like they had been dyed green at Woodstock, disoriented me a bit.

"My foot's stuck," he repeated, tugging at his leg as if to prove it. Finally I came to my senses and helped him move one of the boulders enough for him to slip free. The stones were big; I didn't see how anyone could have gotten a foot between them in the first place unless they simply materialized there.

"Like, thanks, bro'," he said, rubbing his ankle. He reached out to shake my hand. "The name's Mike." I shook his hand.

"My name..."

"Yeah, I know. You're Kenn. I know all about you, man. You were picked." He started rubbing his foot again. "Just like me."

He flexed his ankle while I stood there speechless, watching him. This had to be someone's idea of a bizarre joke.

"No damage done," he said, putting some weight on his foot. "We've never tried that before. Could have been worse. I could have come together inside a rock or something."

"Who are you?" I was too surprised to be tactful. He laughed. It was an easy, confident laugh.

"You mean what am I, don't you? I'm a Greenie. 'Little Greenies,' I think you call us. We're the guys in electricity, the brothers boogyin' down those wires, lighting your bulbs, frying your burgers. Your brain was scrambling trying to picture an electron and you said the magic word. So, here I am."

"Aren't you a little...big?" He laughed again.

"Like, this probably seems a little off-the-wall to you, doesn't it? Like, I'm probably weirding you out. Usually I'm real small. This is a first. I don't know exactly how, but they changed me so I'd be more like you. 'Anthropomorphosizing,' I think they called it. It's supposed to be temporary." He grinned with very white teeth and crossed his fingers.

I sat down on a rock and reached for another beer. Just to be friendly, I offered him one too, even though I was pretty sure I was in the middle of some sort of heat-induced hallucination.

"No can do, bro', wrong dimension. But it's a good idea. The first communication between man and Greenie. That's like history. We ought to have a brew together. Slop some suds."

He reached behind the boulder and pulled out his own six-pack, opened a can, and drained it down. "Right on!" he said, wiping his green mouth with the back of his green hand. "Sock it to me!"

I just stared out at the glassy lake and wondered what I had eaten that might have been bad. Mike was happy just to sit there not saying much, drinking his beer and watching the birds. He seemed very real.

There was no easy way to start this conversation. "If electricity is really you little Greenies, why haven't you made contact before?" I asked.

"Hey, why haven't you guys tried to contact us? Anyway, we just found out that humans exist. We managed to pick up a couple of your television programs, and finally figured out how to de-code them."

"So that's how you learned English?"

"Right on, man! We learned everything about you humans from just three TV shows. First, of course, there was "Dobie Gillis," with that smooth cat Maynard G. Krebbs. Then we picked up on "Laugh-In" and "Saturday Night Live." It's all we needed, if you can dig it.

Totally. Now we're working on de-coding some musical show about a gong which ought to help even more."

"You learned English by watching "Dobie Gillis" and "Laugh-In?"

He smiled and nodded, proud of that accomplishment.

"A lot of Greenies still don't believe in you humans, though. That's part of the reason I was sent. I'm supposed to get evidence. Do you have any ideas?"

"If they don't believe in humans," I asked, "What do the rest of the Greenies believe in?" In unison, like spectators at a tennis match, we turned to watch a bird gliding low over the water looking for fish.

"It's weird, man," he said. "They've got this fairy tale to explain all the strange things you folks do. They call it the electron theory.

I just nodded, and we didn't talk any more. Didn't need to. We understood each other. The sun sank below the horizon and we watched the twilight uncover all the colors that had been hiding in the clouds. The sky faded from blue, to orange, to gray, and finally to deep velvet black. Mike the Greenie and me, the human, fell asleep without noticing that we were sleepy, like little boys at summer camp.

If I had dreams that night, of any kind, I've forgotten them.

Birth of a Prophet

"Why do you call yourselves Greenies?" The sun had risen, and I was frying a couple of fresh trout over the campfire.

"Actually," Mike said slowly, "You were the one to call us Greenies. The name we call ourselves does not translate well. But our scientists could tell, somehow, that you were on the right track. Anyway," he said, pulling his T-shirt up to expose a flat green belly, "We're green."

"But, in my theory, you were invisible."

"That makes it tougher, of course," he said, "But hey, I believe you also said we're imaginary. I don't feel imaginary, but I guess it's possible. If you're imaginary, man, you can be whatever color you want. And I want to be green."

23

"Maybe I just don't understand. You're green, and you're invisible. You exist, and yet you're imaginary?"

"Hey, man," he said, "If you can't handle the truth, you can always go back to the electron theory."

I just nodded and we ate the trout in silence. Contradictions had never stopped any other scientific theory, I thought. And, after all, he was right there beside me, a green hippie who appeared out of nowhere from another dimension. It was a pretty compelling argument. I did find it curious that he could eat my trout, but he couldn't drink my beer. I decided it was a minor philosophical annoyance. We talked all morning.

I learned that Mike was a messenger and pioneer of sorts. His mission was to explain to me what electricity really is, and why it does the things it does. I had been chosen to receive this message, to be a sort of prophet who would teach this truth to the world.

I told him I'd rather just fish. He shrugged.

"It's up to you man. I'll lay it out for you, you do what you want. But it's a pretty low-key gig. Nobody'll believe you anyway."

"Then why bother?"

"Oh, sooner or later they'll dig it. It's a human tradition, as far as we can tell. One guy figures things out, he gets ridiculed and usually killed. They sock it to him. After a while, everyone says, 'Hmm... old dead what's-his-name had a good idea, didn't he? Maybe we ought to try that.' Then they use his idea, make a lot of money, and name a wing of the library after him."

"You make it sound like a lot of fun."

"Hey, we don't figure they'll kill you. They'll be cool. We figure they'll call you crazy, say you're not a totally hep cat. Then they'll put you on the late night talk shows and let you drift into oblivion. You'll be small potatoes. It's not like you'll be suggesting nationalizing the utility companies, or cutting the tobacco subsidy."

"I don't know..."

"Look, no robes or anything. Keep the sneakers. You don't even have to talk. Just write it down somewhere, like in a diary or something. Fifty years from now, who knows? Maybe you'll be famous. Anyway, I got to tell you what I know before I split. Otherwise, I can't get back. And I got this chick back there…" His eyes rolled upward and his smile told the rest. How could I resist? I couldn't keep him from his Little Greenie sweetie.

"Okay, Okay, no promises. But I'll listen."

Mike pulled a trout out of the pan and grinned. "Dreamsville, daddy-o! Too much!"

I didn't have the heart to tell him that no one talks like that anymore.

Voltage and Motivation: Greenies Do Things For Reasons

"Greenies like to party," Mike said. "It's what we live for. And a party means girls, beer, and rock 'n roll. If there's a bunch of Greenies cruising down a wire, you can bet we're headed for a party."

"Am I supposed to be writing this down?" I asked. This was a new role for me. Mike and I were sitting by the lake fishing. He had somehow come up with the neatest fishing pole I'd ever seen. It was long, glossy black, and made a low whirring sound whenever he cast.

"Nah," said Mike. "You can't write and fish at the same time. Let's just mellow out and get on the same wavelength. Let the heavy stuff slide for a while."

"Right," I said, suppressing an urge to either say, "Like right," or "Right on."

"Anyway," he continued, "When Greenies party, it works like this: the chicks buy kegs of beer and turn up their radios. The brothers hear that rock 'n roll, get in their little green cars and motovate toward the music. Works every time."

"Don't the girls ever drive toward the guys?"

"No, man, that's not the way it works. The chicks buy the beer and we chase 'em. We hear that music and the urge comes over us. We call it the "need-to-party." Suddenly he put down his pole, went over to the boulder he had appeared behind, and came back with a book. "It's a Greenie-English dictionary," he said. "You know, for translating.

Let's see, need-to-party…Oh, yeah, here it is: 'voltage.' We call it the need-to-party, you call it voltage. Does that make sense to you?"

"Well, sort of," I said slowly. "Voltage is supposed to be electrical pressure. Electromotive force, they sometimes call it. If you have a lot of electrons in one place, they'll repel each other. That's because they all have a negative charge. They'll be attracted to a positive charge. The amount of attraction is called voltage. If you have a lot of electrons in one place and very few in another there's a lot of voltage between the two places. Voltage is also called 'potential,' because whenever you have that situation you have the potential of electrons moving to equalize their numbers in the two spots. Basically, voltage is electrical pressure."

Mike just stared at me.

"That's what they teach you?"

I nodded, and he shook his head.

"That's heavy, man. You got to can all that stuff. Voltage is like…" He paused, searching for a word. His face brightened. "Desire. That's pretty good. Or motive. It's the reason we move. Whether we can get to the party or not, voltage is how much we want to go." He shook his head in disbelief. "Electromotive force! What do they think, we're like water in a pipe, and voltage is the water pressure that forces us through?"

"Well," I said, "Actually I have heard that analogy used before…"

"This may be harder than I thought." Mike stared into the distance. The sun was reflecting off all the tiny wind-waves on the surface of the lake, the birds and insects were settling into their mid-day song routines. I thought I saw his fishing line twitch just a little.

"Electricity is Greenie dudes making tracks for those Greenie babes. And voltage is the reason we go. It's our need-to-party. It's our thirst for brew. It's the big itch that must be scratched. It's a lot more like hunger than it is like water pressure."

"I've never heard it explained quite like that before."

"I can dig it, man, but I got to tell it like it is. Say you got a flashlight battery. On the positive side of that battery you got a bunch of Greenie chicks. And, I mean, some of those chicks are *very* positive. On the negative side, you got some Greenie dudes. Those chicks, they buy a couple kegs and turn up their little boom boxes. Us guys, we hear the music, and right away we feel that need-to-party. The more chicks there are, the more little boom boxes they got, which makes that music loud. That means more dudes hear it and feel that need-to-party. If there's a way for us to get there, we're gonna cruise. If all the bridges are down and the roads are closed, maybe we can't get there. But we're still gonna feel that urge. That's what voltage is: It's boy Greenies feeling that need-to-party and girl Greenies playing rock 'n roll. Voltage is that hunger to be movin' on down the road."

That all seemed pretty far-fetched to me. "Gosh, Mike," I said, trying to be diplomatic. "Most of the books I've read say that the negative side of a battery has excess electrons, giving it a negative charge. The positive side of the battery hasn't got as many electrons as it has protons, so it has a positive charge. The excess electrons are attracted to the positive side of the battery. Given a route, they'll travel toward it. Voltage is supposed to be the difference in those charges that causes the attraction."

Mike just laughed. At that moment, the tip of his pole jerked toward the lake. He yelled out some expression I'd never heard before and began playing a fat rainbow trout. Obviously, my education would have to wait.

The Woodstock of Voltage

The first dream didn't make me nervous. It was natural, even pleasant. I was floating effortlessly through a dense swirling fog. Somehow I knew that I was a great distance above the ground, and the fog around me was really a cloud. The wind lifted me like a feather, but I felt no sense of danger, no urgency or unease. I could have been a drop of water, comfortable in familiar surroundings.

Gradually I became aware that someone else was also floating in the cloud, but I couldn't see them clearly. I tried to shout a greeting, but, in my peaceful, sleepy condition, that required more effort than I could muster. I closed my mouth again and waited. The wind tossed me more vigorously, but it didn't frighten me. It was fun. I found myself laughing like a trusting baby being tossed around by his mother. The other figure moved closer as the wind tossed him, too, and I could see that it was Nick Scott, my best friend in first grade. I can't remember now if he looked grown up or not, and it didn't seem to matter at the time. It was Nick, all right, and though we hadn't seen each other for years, he recognized me at once and grinned. A happy warmth filled me. There was a lot of catching up to do, a lot of questions I wanted to ask old Nick, and I didn't know where to start. Nick nodded, as if he understood, and neither of us spoke. It was enough just to be together again.

Now I could see that there were other boys and men floating in the cloud, too. As they drifted close, I recognized old friends I hadn't seen in a long time. Each one smiled and nodded when they saw me. They kept appearing out of nowhere until there were thousands of us, floating together, riding crazy up-drafts and sliding down invisible thermal hills like children at some bizarre amusement park.

Then I heard a familiar throbbing sound somewhere in the distance, too faint to be sure of. The men around me stopped moving and became alert, cocking their heads, straining to hear it, too. It grew louder and I could distinguish drums, then an electric guitar, and finally a familiar voice singing. It was Chuck Berry doing *Johnny B. Goode*.

Now, *Johnny B. Goode* is one of those songs I can't resist. My foot starts tapping at the thought of it. It affects me like a drug, or magic. When I hear it, I want to be on the dance floor, right next to the biggest speaker, flailing around like an octopus on a fish hook. Of course, when I heard it now, I moved toward the sound and so did all the guys around me. The sound came from somewhere below the cloud.

The bottom edge of the cloud was flat and abrupt, like a floor, and as far as my eyes could see it was covered with men and boys, floating and staring eagerly at the ground far below. There was a huge green meadow down there, with a stage in the middle of it. Chuck Berry Himself was playing with an all-star band, and he was really smokin'. He was burning up that stage as if he were 19 years old again and still had something to prove. He sang like he owned the world and all the good things in it, and rock 'n roll was the part of his kingdom he loved the best.

A huge crowd had gathered. With a start I realized that there were no men in that audience. Only beautiful women, dancing and clapping in time to the music, shaking their hair and laughing with each other. I'd never seen so many people having such a good time. Suddenly a powerful feeling swept over me. I had to be down there. I had to be dancing. Nothing else in the world mattered, nothing else was real. There was only a burning hunger to be part of that crowd, part of the music. But it was much too far below me. There was no way to get there. My mouth went dry and I started to sweat. I ached to join the celebration.

From out of nowhere a green figure appeared beside me. "Can you feel it?" Mike asked. I could only nod. "It's cool, man. That's what I was telling you about. That's the need-to-party. You call it voltage. All these guys are feeling it. When there's enough voltage, they'll jump. You will too. Watch this!"

Mike put his arms up in the air, crouched and dived toward the ground. I was terrified, as I watched him plunge almost in slow-motion. But when he finally hit the ground, instead of being smashed to bits, he bounced as if he'd landed on some huge trampoline and started coming back up. When he was nearly back to the cloud, someone else jumped, and the two of them fell together to the meadow only to bounce back once more. This time a dozen guys jumped with them. Pretty soon, thousands of men were diving from the cloud and bouncing off the meadow like a column of tennis balls. It didn't seem to hurt them, and I couldn't wait any longer. I leaped for the meadow.

Somehow Mike was there again, falling right with me.

"Lightning, man," he said. "You're doing lightning. You just can't hold back that much need-to-party."

"This is a weird dream," I muttered, and woke up just before I hit the ground.

Voltage: The Short Version

Voltage is the force that pushes electricity, the reason it moves, or wants to move. The word "voltage" hasn't got any special Latin meaning or anything. It simply honors an early scientist named Volta. Voltage is measured in units called volts. A flashlight battery might have a volt or two. Lightning might have a million volts.

Voltage is sometimes called "potential" because whenever there is voltage there is the potential for electricity to move. If you say something has a lot of electrical potential, that is the same as saying it has a lot of voltage. There does not have to be any electricity actually moving to have voltage. There need only be the potential for movement.

Voltage is also sometimes referred to as "electromotive-force" which is abbreviated "emf." Same stuff, new phrase. In formulas, voltage is usually represented by a capital "E."

Of course, you and I know that voltage is really "a group of Greenies' need-to-party" or their "Enthusiasm." This is also abbreviated "E" which is a handy coincidence.

If you refuse to believe in Greenies (or if you're captured and interrogated) say that voltage is the difference in the number of electrons between two points.

Current:
There Are Millions of Greenies Pounding on the Gates, Sir, and They Want to Hold an Election

"Weird dream," I said again as I woke up and rubbed my eyes. Mike was studying his little dictionary, and I could smell trout frying over the campfire. Mike was muttering to himself, and as soon as he realized I was awake, he began talking to me.

"Current!" he said in disgust. "Another dumb word! What do they think we are, drops of water or something?"

"Well…" I began.

"Don't answer, man. I don't think I want to know."

"Give me a better word," I said. "Better than that, give me a cup of coffee." I sat up as he handed me a cup of boiled coffee. I ignored the floating grounds and he ignored my sleepiness.

"Traffic, that's a better word. Little Greenies in their little green cars cruising toward the party. If there's lots of little cars, you say there's lots of current, we say there's lots of traffic."

"And that's different from voltage?"

"Oh yeah, man. Remember, voltage is the need-to-party, the desire, the motivation. It's the reason you get into your car. Current is how much traffic is actually moving down the road. You'd never confuse your thirst for a beer with the number of cars on the road, would you? Well, that's the difference between voltage and current. Different birds, man, different birds. If you had a bunch of cars parked on a steep hill, they'd all want to be moving down that hill. That steep hill is like voltage. It's the thing that pushes the cars. If a driver takes his foot off the brake, his car is going to roll down that hill. It becomes current. If there's lots of cars rolling, there's lots of current."

"I don't know, Mike," I said, sipping the coffee through my teeth to strain the grounds. "I was taught that current is the movement of electrons. If a lot of electrons are moving, we say there's a lot of current."

"Whatever works for you, man. I can dig it. I bet they count these imaginary electrons, too, and have another goofy jargon word for how much current there is, right?"

He had me again.

"They don't actually count each electron, of course, " I said, a little defensively. "But they do measure current. They can tell how much electricity is flowing through a wire. The unit of measurement is the ampere."

"Am-peer, eh?" Mike sort of grinned as he exaggerated the pronunciation. "Am-peer, am-peer; I kind of like that. I knew a girl once named Ampere. Greenest skin you ever saw. Everyone called her Amp, for short. Did they name the thing after some human girl?"

"Well, no. Ampere is not a common girl's name. Actually it was named after a man."

"A man! Wow, I bet he got teased in school!"

"It was a long time ago. Anyway, I think it was his last name. Current is measured in amperes, but sometimes we shorten that down to amps, just like the girl you knew did. You might say 'There's 10 amps of current flowing through that wire,' or 'The fuse will blow if two amps of current go through it.'"

"And do you have ampere jams when everyone gets off work at the same time and clog up the highways?"

"No, we call them traffic jams. We reserve the word ampere for electricity."

"Hmm," he said.

I took a deep breath and sorted the words in my head. Voltage is the force behind electrical movement. Current is the movement of electrons, or Greenies, or whatever, through something. Electricity can have both voltage and current at the same time, and usually does. We measure voltage in volts and current in amperes or amps. So, we might say something has 10 volts of potential and five amps of current flowing and everyone would know what we were talking about.

Even Mike would know. I could tell he thought our expressions were a little funny, and that kind of irritated me. I hadn't made fun of all his absurd attempts to talk like an American. Anyway, he was teaching me about electricity, and electricity is supposed to be a serious subject isn't it?

Yes. It certainly is.

Lake Dubious

High on a mountain sits a vast, cold and foggy lake. Two rivers leave Lake Dubious and wander down the mountainside to the ocean far below. One of the rivers is mighty, like the Nile, or the Mississippi. It is deep and wide, filled with huge, silent fish, and is used by water-skiers and houseboats. The other river is tiny, only a few inches deep and only a few feet wide. It's really just a creek. You can see the rocks you step on when you wade across it.

Lake Dubious is exactly one mile higher than sea level. Regardless of the twists and turns either river takes, they each transport water one vertical mile over the course of their journey to the sea. The one mile difference in elevation between the lake and the sea is the reason the water flows down either river. Any drop of water in that lake has a potential fall of one mile in its future. This difference in elevation is the liquid equivalent of voltage.

Both rivers have the same voltage. They each have that same one mile difference in elevation from beginning to end. They are not identical rivers, however. One has a lot more water in it. The big river has more amperes of current. Because of this, the big river can do more work than the small river. It can carry larger ships, move large boulders that happen to fall into it, and turn a much larger water-wheel. Current is the muscles of electricity.

If you're looking for an electrical river to be your body-guard, choose one with many amperes.

Either river can move sand to the ocean. If moving sand is the job at hand, you have to know how much voltage is available, and also how much current. If you have more voltage, you'll move more sand. If you increase the current flow, you'll also move more sand. Since both the Lake Dubious rivers have the same voltage or potential, other variables account for their differences. Things like the size of their channels, whether they meander or plunge, or if either one is obstructed.

The work that electricity does is measured in "watts." Watts is simply voltage times current. If 10 amps of current are flowing, and you know you're using a 12-volt battery to push that current, then you are using 120 watts.

The power company charges you for the work their electricity does. They charge you for however many watts you use each month. Their meters measure the actual work done by electricity in your home. Your bill is based on how much sand you moved, and how far you moved it.

Meeting Some Resistance

"Resistance, now that's a pretty good word. Opposition to current flow. Anything that makes it harder to boogy on down the road." Mike was studying his little dictionary again as I returned to camp. He hadn't even looked up, but just started talking. I was in a good mood because I'd caught several real beauties. I had always thought of 'resistance' as a political word, so I was a little confused again, but Mike just went on talking while I cleaned the fish. They really were nice fish, I thought.

"Remember," he said, "that current is like traffic. Greenies feel the need-to-party, jump in their little green cars and cruise. But there's all kinds of roads, man. Some are smooth, straight and easy to drive. They don't offer much resistance to traffic. Other roads are rotten. If it's tougher to drive, there's more resistance."

"Like a dirt road?"

"Right on! A dirt road has more resistance than a super-highway. Takes more work to go down it. A road covered with four feet of snow has a lot of resistance. If you don't have a desperate need-to-party, you won't even try to start the car."

"So resistance is green snow on the highway of life?"

"Well, yeah, I guess it is. But there's different kinds of resistance. Different materials are easier to travel through than others. Things that are easy to move through are called conductors. Metals are usually good conductors. They have very little resistance. If something has a lot of resistance, we call it an insulator. Wood is a bad conductor, a good insulator. Lots of resistance. Very tough to boogy through wood."

"I've found that to be true, myself," I said. "But you know, Mike, all the books say that a good conductor is something that has a lot of free electrons, while a good insulator doesn't."

"Well, shoot, I guess you better believe it then," Mike said with a serious face. "I didn't realize it had actually been written down in a book. It must be true. I know several million little Greenies that are going to be very disappointed, though. They'll be sitting in their little green cars looking for a highway and only finding a jumble of free electrons."

"I didn't mean to say…"

Mike interrupted my apology with a wave of his hand and a smile.

"Doesn't matter. I know you've got to tolerate all these mythologies. The important thing to remember is that electricity travels pretty easily through a conductor but, unless it has an awful lot of voltage, it won't go through an insulator. The less resistance a material has, the easier it is for electricity to go through it.

"But there's other ways to create resistance," he went on. "For example, which has more resistance, a big wire or a small wire?"

"Well," I said, "The big wire has more metal for the current to go through, so I guess it has more resistance."

"Wrong!" Mike was gleeful. "If you have a thousand cars to move from one city to another, will it be easier to go down a six lane interstate highway, or a one lane road?"

"That's obvious."

"Same with electricity. A small path is tougher to move a lot of Greenies through, so it has more resistance than a big path. Resistance can be a physical bottleneck, a very thin wire, something like that. Here's another one: Which has more resistance, a long wire or a short wire?"

I thought for a moment, not wanting to look foolish again, but knowing that logic alone wasn't going to explain Greenies any better than it explained electrons.

"I guess," I said slowly, "If you've got a thousand cars to move down a road, it would be harder to go a hundred miles than a hundred feet. You'd use up more gas, your drivers would get tired; pretty much in every way it would be harder. If current is like traffic, I'd say a long wire has more resistance than a short wire."

"Now you're catching on. A long wire does have more resistance than a short wire, and a skinny wire has more resistance than a fat one. Not much to it, bro'. A thing's resistance to current is determined by its size and shape and by what it's made of."

"And the more resistance there is, the fewer Greenies will go through it?"

"Basically, yeah. The amount of need-to-party affects the traffic, and the road conditions also affect the traffic."

"What you're saying is, if voltage increases, current also increases; but if resistance increases, the current decreases?"

Mike sat there thinking for a minute.

"Gosh, Kenn," he said at last. "I never thought of it that way before. But I think you're right." He started leafing through his little dictionary again.

"And the unit of measurement...let's see here...Oh yeah. Resistance is measured in 'ohms.' Ten ohms isn't much resistance. A million ohms is a lot."

"Hmm," I said.

"No man, not 'hmm'. It's 'ohm'. Resistance is measured in ohms."

"Oh," I began, but he misunderstood again.

"No man, pay attention. Ohms! Ohms! Resistance is measured in ohms!"

This time I just nodded.

Oh, Give Me a Home...

In the dream I was a buffalo, in the middle of a vast herd of buffaloes, and all of us were green. Several of us stood on a road near a sign that said, "This Way To Party." For as far as I could see, the prairie was dotted with green buffaloes standing around in the sunshine, chewing grass, making up poetry, doing buffalo stuff. I tried to do whatever they did and hoped they couldn't tell I was not a life-long bison.

Suddenly I heard faint music. It came from far down the road. Oh, no, I thought. Not *Johnny B. Goode!* I couldn't help myself; I immediately began walking toward it, trying to look casual. A few of the other shaggy creatures could also hear the music and began walking with me.

As the music got louder, many more of my bovine companions heard it and joined the procession. Shoulder to green furry shoulder, an army of these instinctive party animals moved toward that music like a huge rolling shag carpet.

Then the road ended at a steep canyon. We couldn't get across, but we could still hear the music, louder than ever. I discovered that buffaloes have a very intense need-to-party, and can get rather single-minded when it is aroused. They were peeved that they could not get past that canyon. It became obvious that things would not be pleasant if a solution was not found. I did not want to be handy if their playful mood turned nasty. When I suggested we all just go munch on some sagebrush and play Twenty Questions, a number of them turned toward me with suspicion in their beady little eyes.

Luckily, someone discovered a foot bridge before things got out of hand. The bridge was only wide enough for a single-file line, so one by one we began to cross. I didn't like the bridge. The canyon was deep, the bridge swayed. The vast army of snorting, hairy animals behind me pawed at the dust in their impatience and waited their turns. Deep down I knew that I wasn't like them, and that also made me nervous. The music was loud, the need-to-party was so strong you could smell it in the air. At least, I think that's what I could smell. The bridge allowed a few buffalo to make it past the canyon, but it restricted traffic greatly. Where hundreds of buffalo could travel down the road, only a single line could travel across the foot bridge. That one bottle-neck reduced all the party traffic for miles. Of course, if they turned down the music, I sensed that some of the buffaloes would lose interest pretty fast, and traffic would be even further reduced. The fellows farthest from the party wouldn't hear it. It seemed odd that both the volume of the music and the size of the footbridge could affect how many buffalo went to a party.

As I made my way across the bridge, (as carefully as is possible for a buffalo) I kept thinking that something was missing, like someone was trying to tell me something but my furry ears couldn't understand.

I woke up before I reached the party. For some reason, I couldn't get a phrase out of my head: When voltage increases, so does current. But, as resistance increases, current decreases.
It didn't seem to have much to do with buffalo.

Body Heat

Every time electricity fights its way through something that has resistance, heat is produced. The more current, the more heat. Also, the more resistance, the more heat. Since everything electricity goes through has some resistance, everything heats up, at least a little. A copper wire has less resistance than an iron nail, so if the same amount of current is flowing through them both, the nail will get hotter. A thin nail has more resistance than a thick one, so it will produce more heat. Air has a lot of resistance, but if you can provide enough voltage, electricity will even go through air. When it does, it creates a tremendous amount of heat. That's part of the fun of lightning, and why it can fry telephone poles so quickly. Much heat, produced by much current going through much resistance.

The fact that electricity always produces heat when it moves through resistance is extremely handy. The devices that heat our waterbeds, broil our steaks, toast our bread and zap insects on our patios all rely on the heat produced by electricity going through resistance to do their jobs. In the case of the unfortunate flying insect, its own body provides the necessary resistance. If an electrical device is producing heat, some current is probably moving through some resistance.

Heat produced by resistance is one of the most common and valuable products of electricity. Unwanted heat is also one of the principle causes of equipment failure. The heat created by electrical devices as an unavoidable by-product routinely melts and fries critical components. When heat is not the desired product (in a motor or computer, for example) the energy that is converted to heat is wasted and contributes to the inefficiency of the device. In many cases,

38

enough heat is produced incidentally that equipment must be designed with a provision for cooling.

We all agree on this: Electricity produces heat as it travels through resistance. Why it does so is more of a mystery. It could be that electrons give up energy as they are forced to move from their normal nuclear orbits. More likely it's that Greenies get angry when road conditions make it difficult to get to a party and their temperatures (and blood pressures) rise. The more Greenies there are, and the more difficult the road conditions, the more heat.

Believe whatever mythology makes you comfortable, but remember this: Add more resistance, you'll get more heat. Add more current, and you're also going to get more heat. Of course, by adding more resistance you're going to reduce the amount of current, so the total amount of heat might not change. However, you can concentrate its location. If you've got a long stretch of super-highway interrupted by a cliff and foot bridge, it's easy to see where most of the buffalo cursing and swearing is going to be. Right on that footbridge, where the pressure from the rear causes a lot of painful horn wounds on your sensitive buffalo caboose at the same time that the herd ahead of you seems to be purposely trying to keep you from the party.

There are many angry phrases that don't translate well from buffalo-Greenie to English, but their general meaning is pretty universal. You will understand these phrases and learn to appreciate the heat produced by resistance the next time you try to change a light bulb with your bare hand without letting it cool down first.

Circuits, Switches, Ants, Lizards and Pigs

This has always bothered me: If the negative terminals of batteries have excess electrons (a negative charge) and the positive terminals of batteries have too few electrons (a positive charge) and opposites attract, why can't I hook a wire between the negative side of one battery and the positive side of a different battery and get any current?

The truth is it won't work. No current will flow. Had someone been able to explain that to me, I probably would never have written this book. I would have accepted the electron theory into my life with gratitude and respect for its inventors. If you like to watch people squirm, ask a science teacher to explain this to you. See if they can satisfy you without mentioning Greenies. Give them a time limit so they don't try to wear you down with jargon.

To get current to flow, there has to be a return path, a closed loop, a "circuit." A wire between the negative and positive sides of the same battery creates a "complete circuit," and current will flow through it like crazy until the battery is worn out. The word "circuit" means a path that finally returns to the spot it started from without any interruptions. If you ever want to do more than zap cat noses, you've got to fool with circuits.

A circuit requires a source of voltage like a battery. Current leaves the negative side of the battery, makes its way through a conductor and perhaps through other items like a light or a toaster, and then returns to the positive side of the battery. A device for interrupting this loop is called a "switch." The circuit is the pathway that electricity takes, including excursions through switches and other devices, until it finally returns to the voltage source.

If electricity can't flow through the circuit because the path is incomplete or broken, we call it an "open" circuit. If the loop is complete, we say it is a "closed" circuit. Remember, it only takes one break in the pathway, one "open," to stop current from moving through all parts of the circuit. That's why a switch works. By interrupting current in a one-inch section of a circuit, a single switch can control whether or not current flows through a thousand Christmas tree lights. In addition to open circuits and closed circuits, you will also hear the phrase "short circuit." A more reasonable phrase would have been "short cut." That's what it is. If there is an opportunity for Greenies to take a short cut to the party without fooling with whatever work you have planned for them later in the circuit, they will "short out" or short circuit. They'll take the easy path, the short path, the path of least resistance, even if no work whatsoever gets done.

The words "open" and "closed" confuse people. Current will flow through a closed switch but not an open one. Perhaps a complicated mathematical formula and a few words in Latin would make it more memorable.

Just kidding. How about a cute little picture story?

You are an ant, walking along the top of a wire fence.
The fence encloses a square field, and has one gate.
If the gate is closed, you walk right over it,
Around the field, returning to your starting place.

Greenies walk inside the wire beneath your feet,
You can hear them whispering to each other.
If the gate is closed, the Greenies will also walk around the field,
Over the closed gate and back to their starting place.

If the gate is open, the farmer's pig will escape.
Being an ant, you don't care about that,
But now you can't get around the field.
You stand on that last fence post, crying little ant-tears,
Until a lizard crawls up the fence post and eats you.

If the gate is open, Greenies can't get across, either.
But lizards don't care for Greenies, so they leave them alone.
The fence is a circuit, the gate is a switch
The farmer and the pig are imaginary,
The lizard teaches the electron theory at a local college.

Magnetism

Guys who believe in the electron theory don't like to talk about magnetism. It is a major source of their personal insecurity. We have known for a long time that electrical current is always surrounded by a magnetic field. We also know that whenever a magnetic field moves past a conductor it creates an electric current, but that's about all we know. Einstein spent the last thirty years of his life trying to come up with a "Unified Field Theory" which would have explained why this happens. Unfortunately, being a child of his times, he believed in electrons, couldn't make it work, and died a miserable failure. If only someone would have told him about Little Greenies!

I like to think of magnetism as the wake that Greenies make as they race through Greenie air.

Picture a duck, a green duck named Bruce, with a wild look in his eyes and somewhat disheveled feathers. A bohemian duck, more interested in parties and sleeping late than in science or routine duck business. If we drop old Bruce into a pond, ripples will spread away from his pathetic squawking self; concentric circles of tiny waves that get fainter as they move away from him.

Enterprising duck that he is, Bruce begins to swim. The ripples that he makes take the shape of a "V" spreading behind him. This is called a "wake." If Bruce maintains a steady speed, the wake maintains a simple shape. The ripples he creates reinforce each other. They look like a V-shaped tail of waves following him but not changing shape or growing.

But of course, they are moving. A motorboat, the equivalent of several million ducks (or having, as we say, "mega-duck power") leaves a tremendous wake behind it. Even though the waves it makes look stationary from a helicopter, they will swamp your canoe if you paddle into them.

The waves will also suck you toward them. When a truck passes you on the highway you can feel the pull of its wake as it tries to draw you in. When a shark swims near the floor of the ocean, its wake sucks up the mud and debris.

And when Greenies move through a wire, their wake acts like a magnet. At least, maybe that's what's happening. It makes some sense, it's easy to picture, and the electron theory doesn't provide any better explanation that you or I could understand. Textbooks are satisfied to say that any time electrons move through a conductor they are surrounded by a mysterious magnetic field. And, anytime a magnetic field moves across a conductor it creates a little electrical current in the conductor. No one seems to care why. No one seems to think it's amazing.

While we have been thinking about electricity and magnetism, Bruce has recruited a bunch of equally crazed ducks and is leading them in single file across the lake. Viewed from above, their wakes now combine to form fairly straight parallel lines on each side of the watery parade. Once again, the lines don't appear to move much. They look like they're standing still.

If more ducks land in the line, their wakes will join the existing standing waves and make it move outward. As ducks get bored and fly away, the standing wave will shrink toward the line of ducks.

If Bruce and the gang repeat their performance under water, they will create three-dimensional ripples. If we could see them, it would look like they were swimming through concentric cylinders of underwater ripples. Any hapless fish that ventures too close will be sucked in by this wake and will probably be eaten by a duck.

Believe me, there's nothing a duck can do that a Greenie can't do better. When Greenies move, they leave a wake in Greenie air that forms standing waves which we call lines of magnetic force, or lines of flux. Only some things in our universe are pulled into this wake. Iron is, for example. Other materials are attracted less strongly. As you increase the current, these lines of force grow larger and stronger. As you decrease the current, these lines of force shrink around the wire. You can see it happen with iron filings on a piece of paper with a wire through it.

Magnetism is unaffected by insulators. You can't box it in with any material. It does prefer some substances, however. Iron, once again, seems to be easier for magnetism to travel through. We can encourage magnetism to go where we want by giving it an iron path. Like most of us, it will tend to take the simplest route, so we can concentrate it by providing it that opportunity. When we put iron near an electrical current, most of the magnetism surrounding the current will go through the iron.

Electrically produced magnetism is called electromagnetism, and electrically produced magnets are called electromagnets. By wrapping loops of wire around an iron bar and running some Greenies through the wire we can create a dandy electromagnet. As long as the current is flowing, we can pick paper clips up off the floor.

People who feel that the universe is symmetrical will be happy to learn this: not only does electricity create magnetism, but magnetism can also create electricity. If you move a magnet near a wire you will generate a tiny voltage within the wire. Any movement will work, as long as the lines of force cut across the wire. Every time a line of force crosses the wire, a little more voltage is created. If you use a very strong magnet, with lots of lines of force, you'll get more voltage than if you use a weak magnet. If you move the magnet very quickly, more lines of force will be cutting across the wire, so you'll get more voltage.

If you wrap wire around a nail or other chunk of metal, then run electricity through the wire, the whole thing will act as a magnet and we call it an electromagnet. Some metals work better than others. Iron works great – as long as current flows, it's a strong magnet, then it quickly reverts to normal. Other materials stay magnetized for a very long time after an encounter with electricty, even years. We call these permanent magnets. Every now and then people find chunks of iron on a mountain or in a mine that are naturally magnetized. We call these "natural magnets" or "lodestones." If you stroke a needle with a magnet, you can "magnetize" the needle. Sometimes you'll magnetize a nail just by hitting it. You can also destroy a magnet by pounding it with a hammer. Interesting creatures, these magnets.

It doesn't matter if your magnet is a natural magnet, a permanent magnet, or an electromagnet. Magnetism is magnetism, and it will create voltage every time those lines of force cut across a conductor. In fact, the magnetism that surrounds any electrical current can cause a second electrical current in a nearby wire, and will do so even if you'd prefer that it wouldn't. But only when the lines of force actually move across the second wire.

Magnetism and electricity are the Clark Kent and Superman of science; like Lois Lane, we may never be able to exactly figure out what's going on, but we sure can tell there's a mysterious relationship between the two. Whenever electricity moves, we find magnetism. Whenever magnetic lines of force move across a conductor, they create voltage. It's almost like they were different costumes on the same character. It's almost like electricity changes into magnetism and then back into electricity…

Of course, it's also like green ducks, making green waves on a peaceful green lake.

Through a Glass, Darkly Green

The moment I woke up, I knew something was different, but I couldn't put my finger on it. The lake was cold, gray, and still, as it was every morning. The sky glowed with faint pre-dawn light and a single bird sang its lonely song from some misty perch in the distance. Early morning in the Utah wilderness is always magical, but this was something different. Everything looked strange and unreal, and my sleepy mind struggled to understand why. Mike was sitting on a rock beside me.

"Don't get uptight, man. It's groovy, you'll dig it. Just go with the flow." His voice was reassuring, as if preparing me for something.

I started to rub my eyes awake, when I realized that my hand was glowing a dull red. Terror quickly drove my sleepiness away. My other hand was also glowing, and so were my feet. In panic, I turned to Mike and realized that his green skin was also suffused with a dull red glow.

"It's Okay, man," he said calmly. "It's infrared. You know, heat. Your body always radiates like this, only now you can see it. Didn't you ever want to see more than light?"

"No!" I said honestly. "I want my old eyes back!"

"In a minute, man. Just relax, let the thing take you. Look over there at those blooming weeds."

Despite my distress, I looked. The flowers were a bright violet, like little colored lights in the grass. But I was pretty sure they weren't radiating heat.

"That's ultraviolet. Just a color of light you can't normally see. The flowers aren't glowing like your hands, just reflecting the little bit of sunlight that's creeping over the horizon. Some insects can see ultraviolet. That's what those flowers look like to them every day. And rattlesnakes can see infrared. Right now you can see both. Isn't it a gas? Look over there!"

A field mouse scampered through the grass and leaves, then stopped. I knew he blended perfectly with his surroundings and normally I would never see him. Today he was a tiny red lighthouse beaming out his location. If rattlesnakes can see infrared, I thought, that mouse's confidence in his camouflage is sadly misplaced.

"Wow!" It was all I could say.

"You know, man," Mike said, "It's a good thing you can only see a little part of the spectrum. If you could see radio waves and television waves and microwaves and heat waves, besides your regular light waves, the world would be so confusing you'd never get out of bed. If you tried to explain what you saw they'd lock you up. It would be like being able to see the wind. On a windy day you'd be blind to everything else."

"Wow!" I said again, looking around me, only half listening. The sky was growing lighter and each cloud was a wild rainbow of dazzling light, a sparkling diamond-studded pillow. The still lake was a kaleidoscope of swirling colors. I was sure I was seeing more than infrared and ultraviolet light.

"The infrared and ultraviolet were just for fun," Mike said. "This is what I wanted to show you." He had taken the battery out of my truck and now was attaching my jumper cables to the terminals.

"Hey, wait, you'll short it out!" I shouted, but it was too late. He attached one end of the cable to the positive terminal, and the other end to the negative terminal.

"Party time, boys," he said softly, and sparks flew from his hand as he made the connection. Immediately the cable seemed to swell up, until it was a fat gray snake leaping from terminal to terminal. Looking closer, I saw that it wasn't the wire swelling at all, but a ghostly column of fog surrounding the wire, darkest and most dense close to the center and fading as it got further away. It was an odd fog. It seemed concentrated in tubular membranes, like concentric sausages skewered by the electric cable. I reached out to touch it, but my glowing red hand went right through without disturbing it in the least. When Mike moved the wire, the fog moved with it, but would not cross itself. Like some eerie water balloon, it simply pushed itself aside.

"What is it?" I asked in awe.

"Magnetism, man. It's the disturbance in Greenie air that we make when we move. That fog is there whenever electricity moves through a wire, only you can't usually see it. It's like the disturbance your truck makes in air when it books on down the highway. You can't see it unless you drive down a dusty road. I just added some dust."

"This is a dream, right?" I felt like I was in the middle of some strange house of mirrors and lights at an amusement park.

"You see those darker lines in the magnetism?" Mike asked. I had noticed them already.

"You mean the things that look like tube-shaped bubbles inside each other?"

"Yeah. The layers of concentrated fog. Those are lines of magnetic force, or lines of flux. If we turn up the current, those will grow outward from the wire. When I disconnect the battery, like this…"

He pulled one end of the cable off the battery. Like a ghostly genie disappearing into its bottle, the gray magnetic fog shrank around the wire. In the blink of an eye, it was gone.

"Is that cool, or what?" Mike beamed.

"Infinitely cool," I agreed. "But you don't mean that every single wire in the world is surrounded by a magnetic field like this do you? I mean, you're just making this happen with some trick."

"The only trick is that I'm letting you see the thing, man. Every single wire in the world is surrounded by a magnetic field just like this one, as long as Greenies are cruisin' through it. The more current in the wire, the stronger the field, but even tiny little currents, like in your watch, are surrounded by a tiny magnetic field. Look over there."

He pointed to some power lines strung on poles. The lines were wrapped in the same gray fog, much larger and darker than the one Mike had made with my truck battery. They seemed to flicker and move. I turned to ask about that, but Mike was already over by the truck, putting the battery back into it. I walked toward him.

"The other thing that's cool," he said, over his shoulder, "Is that every time a wire passes through a magnetic field, a current of electricity starts moving through the wire. And not just wires. Any conductor."

"How about squirrels?"

"What?"

47

"There's a squirrel on that power line. Is the magnetic field causing a current in his body. Or aren't squirrels conductors?"

Mike laughed.

"You bet. He's lucky that his body is not a good conductor, though. It's a pretty small current. But you're right. Every time he moves through that magnetic field, or it moves around him, it's going to cause a little trickle of electricity to move through his body."

The sun was beginning to rise, adding its brilliant yellow to the circus of dancing lights surrounding me; the shimmering blue flowers, the lake and clouds, the red glow coming from Mike and me and all the birds and furry creatures in the weeds. The magnetic fog flickered and squirmed around the power lines like endless phantom worms. My new vision capabilities weren't scary any more. They were fun. The infrared glow that floated like a mist around my hands and face seemed natural. I moved my hands around just to watch it. If people really have "auras" like some of my friends believe, this is what they must look like, I thought.

"And magnetism is like the aura that surrounds electricity," I said out loud.

"You got it," Mike said, picking up his fishing pole. "Let's go catch some breakfast."

A little sadly I realized that my eyes were returning to normal. I sighed and picked up my own pole. The mouse faded to brown invisibility among the dead leaves, the squirrel raced through pure clear air along the power line, the ultraviolet flowers blinked off. Now I could see that they were dandelions, and only yellow.

"That was fun," I said, wondering if we'd do it again sometime.

"Not as fun as fishing," Mike replied, and I think he really meant it.

"I guess it depends on how you look at things," I said.

"Yup," he said. "It all depends on how you look at things."

Ode to Induction

Two electric fans are facing each other.
Turn one on, and it blows on the other.
This wind will make the second fan spin
Even though it's not turned on.
Da doo run run run
Da doo run run.

The motion of the first fan
Induced (or caused) a motion in the second fan
Without touching it.
The second fan will be turning
In the opposite direction from the first fan

We call this "induction."
Da doo run run run
Da doo run run.
Two wires are side by side;
Send some electricity through the first one.
As the current builds up,
Lines of magnetic force spread from it.
They cross the second wire,
And induce, or cause, a current in the second wire
Which moves in the opposite direction
From the current in the first wire.

We still call it induction.
Da doo run run run
Da doo run run.

Once the current in the first wire is steady
The lines of force don't move.
No more current is induced in the second wire.
Turn off the current in the first wire;
The lines of force will shrink around it.

As they shrink, they cut across
The second wire again
And induce a current.
This current will be moving the same direction
As the dying current in the first wire.
Down dooby doo down down.

Induction is what we call it
When growing or shrinking lines of force
That surround an electrical current
Move across a conductor
And cause a second current.
Induction only happens when the lines of force
Grow or shrink; that is,
While the current is increasing or decreasing.
Induction is one current
Causing a second current,
Because of the movement of its magnetic field.
Bop shoo-wop shoo-wop.

Like all fine modern poetry,
This section must be read
About three times
Before it will make
Any sense.
Koo-koo ka-choo.

Mutual Inductance:
Let's Go Surfin' Now, Everybody's Learnin' How

There is a multi-mega-duck motorboat racing across an otherwise tranquil lake, leaving a powerful wake of sparkling white water behind it. The boat is heading north, but the waves it makes are heading south. The waves roll away from the back of the boat and keep moving until they crash against the southern shore, a half a mile away, and ruin the fishing.

If that boat was electricity, those waves would be lines of magnetic force. Greenies use these waves for surfing. They wait on their little bitty surf-boards until a boat goes by, then they quick get on its wake and ride until they, too, crash into the shore in a tangled mass of green legs, cursing and confusion. On a hot summer afternoon you'll often see a few billion little Greenies motorboating across the lake, heading toward a party, while another billion or so Greenie-surf in the opposite direction, riding the waves that the first ones made. Of course, it's a dangerous sport and the surfers tend to interfere with the boat traffic, but it's also fun, the way sky diving must be fun, or the way repairing electrical appliances without unplugging them first must be fun.

Scientists call the sport of Greenie-surfing "inductance" or "induction," but until my new theory, they never knew what it was. All they knew was that if you lay two wires side by side and run an electrical current through the first one, somehow, for just an instant, a current also appears in the second wire, running the opposite direction.

If you resist the idea of Greenies surfing, then you're condemned to this explanation: Current in a wire creates a magnetic field around itself. If this magnetic field moves across another wire, it creates an electrical current in the second wire. When you turn on the current in the first wire, the magnetic field grows outward, moving across any conductor that's close to it and inducing a current in it. Once the primary current reaches full strength and is stable, the magnetic field is also stable. Since the field is no longer moving, it doesn't continue to create a secondary current unless you physically move one of the wires.

When you turn off the primary current, the magnetic field surrounding it quickly shrinks to nothing. In that instant, while it's shrinking, it once again moves across the secondary conductor and creates another momentary current. In an interesting twist of fate, it happens that the secondary current is contrary to the primary: If the current in the primary wire is increasing, the induced secondary current will be heading the opposite direction. If the current in the primary wire is decreasing, both currents will be heading the same direction.

Perhaps you have a cruel sense of humor and enjoy tormenting Greenies. If that's the case, you will be able to take advantage of their love of surfing in a number of sadistic ways.

For example, you might lay two wires side by side, and then run an electrical current through both of them, at the same time, heading the same direction. Each of them will induce secondary currents in the other, heading "the wrong direction." Those secondary currents will have to be overcome before the primary currents can reach full power. The effect is that the wires will act as if they had extra resistance for a moment. Of course, it's really because billions of tiny motor boats are trying to navigate through billions of on-coming green surfers without mangling either their boats or their buddies, but you probably shouldn't explain that to your science teacher.

To increase the effect of inductance, we could put a strip of iron between the two wires. Since magnetic lines of force prefer traveling through iron to traveling through air, they will tend to concentrate near the iron, which is near the wires.

Another way to increase inductance is to increase the length of the wires and put them very close to each other. The current in the first wire could actually induce enough current in the second to light a bulb for an instant without being connected to any source of voltage itself and without touching the first wire. When you turn off the current to the first wire, the bulb in the second circuit will light again, for an instant, while the shrinking lines of magnetic force cut across the second wire. Kind of spooky, isn't it?

The current in the first wire induces a current in the second wire. This current (in the second wire) is surrounded by its own magnetic field. As that field grows or shrinks, it will probably move across the first wire and cause another little current. That current might induce another current and so on. The wires influence each other even though they don't touch. Depending on whether current is increasing or decreasing and the way the conductors are arranged, inductance helps or hinders whatever other current is involved. It's called mutual inductance.

Self-Inductance: The Plot Twists, Turns, and Swamps Many Little Green Surfers

Electricity can go through a very long tangled wire piled on your floor without even thinking about it. No matter the twists, turns, knots, figure-eights or apparent disorganization, if the wire is continuous, electricity will move right through it. As the current moves, it will be surrounded by a magnetic field, which follows the wire exactly, through each twist and turn. Now, you may be asking, what happens when you first turn on the juice to such a wire? Won't the lines of force grow? Won't they cross various other sections of the wire? Won't they induce secondary currents? But wait! (you exclaim). It's all the same wire, only jumbled up. Can a primary current induce secondary currents within a single wire?

You bet your bippy it can! Those of you who read and remember my chapter titles can probably guess what we call this. A primary current causing secondary currents within a single conductor is called swamp water.

Just kidding. It's called self-inductance. Yes, it is possible to careen around a lake in your motorboat such that you have to fight your own waves. And, it is possible for the magnetic field that swells and shrinks around a single wire to intersect a different part of the same wire. If the current we create this way is going the opposite direction as the primary current, the two currents will oppose each other. Since the secondary is never quite as strong as the primary, sooner or later the primary will win out, grow to full strength, the lines of force will stop expanding, and the secondary current will disappear. But for that first moment, our wire seems to have a lot of resistance.

Then you turn off the power. Now the lines of force shrink around the wire. They induce a secondary current once more, as they cross parts of the wire, but since they are moving the opposite direction (shrinking, not expanding) the current they induce also changes direction. Now it moves the same direction as the main current. The dying current induces a secondary current that tends to keep it from dying instead of opposing it. You will be amazed to see your light bulb continue to glow for a moment after you have turned off the switch. Self-inductance keeps the current alive until the lines of force have exhausted themselves.

Self-inductance is most dramatic when a wire is twisted back on itself somehow, so that each line of force must cross the wire several times. For that reason, a coil of wire has lots of self-inductance. However, even a straight wire has to deal with the problem. That's because the tiniest wire is huge compared to a Greenie. When that first brave group of adventurous party-seekers races through the center of the wire, the lines of magnetic force are so small they are actually still inside the wire. As more Greenies follow them, the lines of force swell, but they are swelling, for the first instant, inside the wire. This movement of the lines of force through the wire induces a secondary current, heading backward. The two currents heading opposite directions through the same wire interfere with each other until the primary current, once again, finally wins out.

The opposite thing happens when you turn off the power. The lines of force shrink around the wire and actually shrink through the wire toward its center. As they do, they induce a secondary current that is travelling the same direction as the primary current. Until they disappear completely, the current will keep flowing, even though you turned the darn thing off. The energy that went into creating the magnetic field in the first place was stored in it, and is returned to the wire when the field shrinks away.

Self-inductance opposes a current from getting started. It opposes a current from increasing. To be fair, it also opposes a current from decreasing. Self-inductance opposes any change in current. If you try to increase the current, those lines of force create a current heading backward which gets in your way. If you try to reduce the current, those shrinking lines of force induce a current which aids the primary current, keeping it from dying. If self-inductance had its way, current would never change at all.

Sometimes self-inductance is a pain in the neck and we try to reduce its effects. Other times, if we want to delay a current from getting up to full power, for example, we might add self-inductance. The most common way to increase self-inductance is to simply coil up the wire. The more turns a coil has, the more self-inductance it has, and the longer it takes for current to overcome its effects. With enough loops, close enough together, you could delay those Greenies so long that the party would be over by the time they reached it.

The effect of self-inductance is greatest when the current is building up or tapering off, and becomes insignificant when the current is steady. Time has become a factor. Self-inductance acts like resistance that varies with time. It resists current most in the first instant after you turn on the switch, then subsides as current reaches full strength.

The most important thing to remember is this: Self-inductance opposes any increase or decrease in current.

Capacitance:
A Parking Lot on Lover's Leap

You are a Greenie, cruising down a wire in your little green sports car. Suddenly the road forks. To the left you see a fabulous parking lot, so extensive you can't see the end of it. To the right the highway narrows to a one-lane dirt road, full of boulders and pot holes. From both directions the sound of party music is loud and inviting. You are driving fast, as always, and must decide quickly. What do you do?

It was an easy decision for me. If I can hear party music beyond the parking lot, I figure that there must be an exit on the other side, and easy driving across that wide desert of paving. I don't even hesitate. I gun my little engine and shoot onto that black ocean of asphalt. I'm hearing Chuck Berry. You may be hearing Lawrence Welk, or

Barry Manilow or the rock group AC-DC. Many discerning Greenies love the music of "Cottonwood," an acoustic group to which I belong, and whose CD's are available by special order from enlightened music stores everywhere. I mention this only to strengthen and personalize my electrical analogy.

At any rate, our need to party is great, the wind is whipping through our hair, and our little sports cars are growling softly, like proud young cougars racing after prey. The music gets louder as we drive. We know we're heading in the right direction.

Suddenly the parking lot ends. Instead of an exit, we are horrified to discover a brick wall, massive and impassible. We slam on the brakes. You are probably cursing at me. "You wrote the darn book," I can hear you shout. "You should have been able to predict this!"

As I whine some excuse, the cars behind us slam on their brakes and spread out along the wall. We can hear the music beyond that wall, but we just can't get past it. Gradually that huge parking lot fills up.

It becomes obvious to all of us that there is simply no way to get to the party without going back the way we came. Little green horns begin to honk as tempers flare and we begin the long process of trying to turn around and get out of the parking lot, away from the noise and confusion, and back on our way to the party.

Of course, if a Greenie is cruising down the wire now and comes to the same fork in the road, it looks a lot different. To the right is a dirt road, nasty but passable. To the left he sees a thousand acres of green cars, bumper to bumper, all their horns honking, all their drivers cursing and shaking their little green fists in the air, and trying to get out of the parking lot. A massive electrical demolition derby.

That dirt road starts to look pretty good, doesn't it? Of course, we need to come up with some special jargon-word for "the effect of closed parking lots on traffic." The word is "capacitance." Capacitance is the electrical equivalent of capacity. How many green cars can we entice into our green parking lot trap, and how long can we keep them there? Obviously, a large parking lot has more capacity to store parked cars than a small one. And a good strong brick wall will keep them confined better than a wire fence. Something with a lot of capacitance can store a large electrical charge.

A cloud, for example, can have lots of capacitance. Many little Greenies can gather in a cloud. The air that separates them from the party on the ground is like the brick wall. They can hear the party and they want to go, but air is a good insulator; it's very difficult for electricity to travel through it. (Some of you will say that air has few free electrons. If you found yourself saying that, you must now go back to page one and start reading all over again.)

Back to the parking lot for a minute. Greenies are honking their horns and bashing into each other's fenders. Names are being called, fights are breaking out. Everybody knows that the girls who are the best dancers will all be going steady with some other Greenie long before we can untangle this mess and get to the party.

Suddenly, something changes. More girls must have arrived at the party, because the music gets much louder. "Oh no!" I say to myself. "Not Marvin Gaye doing *Heard it Through the Grapevine!* Nobody can resist that!" Our voltage rises instantly. I mean, we *need* to *party!* A kind of insanity grips us and we actually start driving into the brick wall! Thousands of us, one after another, slam our beautiful little sports cars into that solid brick! It's a tiny body and fender man's dream come true! But somehow, it works. The wall sways, cracks appear... it shudders...then a section of brick collapses. Cars shoot through the gap, widening it. Before long, the gap has grown into a major opening wide enough for dozens of cars to pass through, and the rubble is crushed to dust beneath a million green tires.

Back to the cloud for a minute. When the voltage becomes high enough, even the wonderful insulating properties of air aren't enough. A small stream of electricity works its way toward the ground, twisting and turning to take the easiest electrical path. This stream of electricity passing through the air (which has a lot of resistance) heats it. The heated air has less resistance than the cooler air around it, so much more electricity can travel through it, heating it even further. Of course, this pathway is surrounded by lines of magnetic force growing very quickly from the center of the current. You guessed it. Self inductance. We're going to have a massive current heading back up to the cloud, also heating the air. Then a third induced current, heading back to the ground aided by more Greenies from the cloud. The air in that pathway gets so hot it glows and expands. Every time current flows from the cloud to the ground it induces another current going back up. This happens fast – like a million times per second. The air glows white hot along the pathway the electricity is taking and the air expands explosively. All that current also "charges" the air molecules, or "ionizes" them. That process also produces light, and reduces the resistance of the air.

Lightning represents the failure of a cloud's capacitance.

Clouds have about the most magnificent capacitance of anything, and when it breaks down, it will fry your oak tree for you. Of course, everything has some amount. Every wide spot in the road of a circuit can park a few cars, and the traffic pattern will reflect it. And, of course, every brick wall between the Greenies and the party will tend to accumulate at least a few hopeful (if not bright) young lads, parked and waiting.

You can think of capacitance as both the ability of something to store a charge and the attraction of current to places it can't get through. That is, capacitance is a cat in the circuit waiting to be stroked. It's static electricity, or areas that can store static electricity.

If you direct a current onto something that has lots of capacitance but no electrical path out the other side (like a cat or a "capacitor") current will flow until that something becomes full. Once it's full, or charged completely, no current will flow. It still wants to, it just can't.

Capacitance is the electrical equivalent of false hope, unrequited love, and unrealistic expectations.

Romeo had a lot of capacitance.

Direct Current and Alternating Current

"Direct Current" ought to be the name of a high-powered rock group. It ought to be the name of a hard-fisted detective in some best-selling series of mystery books. It ought to be the name of a secret and powerful cult.

Instead, it refers to one-way traffic. If a circuit is arranged so that electricity flows in one direction through its entire pathway, that current is called direct current, and abbreviated "DC." Direct current is usually produced by batteries and DC generators.

If we employ our vast electrical cunning, we can reverse an electrical current while it is racing toward the inevitable party. That's right. We can stop those Greenies, turn 'em around, and make them race right back the way they came. Switching the wires on the battery would do it, for example. Then, in a cruel mood, we could reverse them again. Back and forth. One instant electricity is headed clockwise around a circuit, the next instant counterclockwise, then clockwise again. A human would get frustrated and decide that no party in the world was worth this kind of abuse. But not a Greenie. Forever hopeful, they hear the music suddenly behind them, they slam on their brakes and turn to race in this new direction. They are admirably persistent and optimistic, if perhaps somewhat slow learners.

Current that keeps reversing its direction like that is called alternating current, or "AC." Alternating current is almost always produced by an "alternator," a device which spins magnets within a coil of wire.

Thomas Edison was a big fan of DC. When he started a company to sell his inventions (perhaps you've heard of it – it's called "General Electric"), he thought that the world would be simpler if everyone used the same kind of current. He thought it should be DC. Because all his little inventions were designed to operate on DC, perhaps his enthusiasm had a less than objective scientific basis.

Nikola Tesla, on the other hand, pointed out one huge advantage that AC has: It doesn't lose as much energy as DC when you send it through very long wires. Of course, Mr. Tesla was famous for his "Tesla Coil" and other alternating current devices and was perhaps no more objective. Still, he had logic on his side, and alternating current has been sold by power companies ever since. In an interesting historical footnote, Mr. Tesla did not start General Electric. He did have a good buddy named George Westinghouse, however.

But that's another story.

Alternating current cannot possibly be understood without some new jargon words. "Cycle" is the first one. Cycle means "round trip." A Greenie leaves Chicago and travels down a wire to Salt Lake City. Then someone switches the battery connections and he races back the same wire to Chicago. That's one round trip, or one cycle. Electrical engineers being what they are will probably reverse the current again, and our boy's headed west again. The cycle begins when a Greenie leaves Chicago and it ends after he's gone to Salt Lake City, turned around, traveled back home to Chicago and is ready to start over. One trip west, then the same trip in reverse, east to the point he started from.

Greenies travel fast. They can complete 60 round trips of that distance in one second.

We don't measure cycles in miles. We just keep track of how often we reverse the direction. If we get in a rhythm and reverse the current 120 times a second, the electricity will make 60 round trips every second. The current is alternating at 60 cycles per second. Each round trip involves reversing direction twice, once in Salt Lake City and once in Chicago. It is so common to use one second as the length of time in this game that no one even bothers to say it any more. "Sixty-cycle AC" means "60 round trips (120 direction reversals) per second." In fact, they usually assume that you understand they're talking about AC, so they don't mention that either. If someone says "a thousand cycles" they aren't talking about a huge motorcycle gang. They mean alternating current that reverses directions 2,000 times per second.

AC is better than DC for long distances because of self-inductance. If you reverse the current before a Greenie has time to get to his destination, you wouldn't think any current would ever arrive in Salt Lake City. On the other hand, with the current constantly increasing, decreasing and reversing, we've got self-inductance coming out our ears, pushing and pulling Greenies on down the line. In this case, self-inductance is one reason the whole thing works.

It is possible to have current that alternates very quickly, thousands and even millions of times per second. Of course, we need a word. The number of cycles per second is called the "frequency" of a current. The frequency of common American household current is just like our Chicago-Salt Lake City current: 60 cycles per second. That's what's flowing through your light bulb right now. The common frequency of household current in Europe is 50 cycles. The frequency of the tiny current in a radio antenna might be 500,000 cycles.

That's not so tough, is it? Direct current travels in one direction, like traffic on a one-way street. Alternating current reverses direction rhythmically. These reversals are measured in "cycles per second" also known simply as "cycles." Each cycle represents a round trip, and includes two current reversals. When we talk about the number of cycles we're talking about frequency. Frequency is measured in "hertz" probably because of the pain involved with reversing directions so quickly at high speeds. Sixty-cycle AC is the same as AC operating at 60 hertz. This is an example of the common scientific practice known as "padding the grant proposal." If you can't think of something new, give something old a second name. Hertz and cycles are the same thing.

Once direct current is at full strength and steady it has the advantage of having little self-inductance to overcome. On the other hand, alternating current is constantly building up, tapering off, switching directions and starting over. Lines of force are constantly moving, so inductance becomes a way of life.

We are wise if we use direct current in situations requiring little inductance and alternating current in situations where we want to use inductance in some way. If you have to transport electricity over long distances, inductance can help you, and you should probably use AC. If you want to avoid producing moving magnetic fields and a bunch of stray secondary currents, stick with DC.

The Magician

I didn't open my eyes or move when I woke up. Something was wrong, terribly wrong. I couldn't hear the lake water lapping on the rocks, or the crickets, or the birds. I was cold and stiff and the ground was too hard. My back hurt, and the air was moist and smelled of mold.

"It is useless to pretend to sleep," a voice snarled. It was the voice of an old man speaking in a loud, harsh whisper. Still I did not move. "Do you think you can fool one such as I so easily?" Even through my closed eyelids I saw a brilliant flash of light. There was a loud crashing sound, like a firecracker or gun. I sat up, startled, and opened my eyes.

I was in a dungeon of some sort, made of solid rock with heavy iron bars across its arched doorway. Everything was damp and musty. I guessed we were deep underground. The only light came from a sickly yellow torch mounted on the wall.

Before me stood the man I would come to know only as "the Magician." He was much taller than I, and extraordinarily thin. He wore a loose, dark blue robe that looked delicately soft and expensive. It also looked perfectly new, as if he had just purchased it an hour ago. His hair was thin, hanging in wispy gray cobwebs down his shoulders and back. His right hand was stretched toward me, and blue smoke rose from his long twig-like fingers. His face was disturbingly unusual. His cheekbones protruded unnaturally and cast shadows on his thin, pale cheeks. His eyes were set deeply into their sockets, as if hiding within two dark caves on a white cliff. From their setting, they moved quickly, flashing tiny reflections of the torch. He was old, I could tell, but radiated the intensity of a young predator.

Perhaps because of his thin appendages, his pale skin, his flashing eyes and the wisps of gray hair floating around his head, the words that instantly flashed through my mind were "like a spider..." I shuddered. All my instincts told me this man was dangerous and probably crazy. Slowly he lowered his hand. Even his movements reminded me of a slow and confident long-legged white spider moving toward the prey its web had captured.

Then he smiled. Like everything else about him, his lips were thin and dry. His smile lacked warmth, and did not comfort me. It was a reptile smile, an executioner's smile and not an expression his face had practiced much. This was a serious fellow. He spoke again in his quiet, rough whisper.

"I trust you have slept well." There was no hospitality in his voice, and he did not wait for me to reply. "I am not a wicked man." I wondered if that was supposed to be comforting. "But I am desperate. You must know that, and understand. If I were not desperate, I would have no interest in torturing you. You must realize it is not personal. Just a thing that must be done."

He cleared his throat. My mind was reeling. Where was I? How did I get here? Who was this frightening old man in the medieval costume? Where was Mike? Why was I here? Did he say torture?

"Your questions will all be answered in good time," he continued, as if reading my mind. "What you must first understand is that your comfort and life are of no interest to me. If you do not prove useful to me, you shall be killed. I don't believe I can be any more direct than that. Do you understand?"

"No, I don't! Where am I? Where…"

Rage filled the Magician's face. Moving faster and more gracefully than I would gave guessed possible, his hand shot out again and pointed at the floor in front of me. Instantly, flames leaped from the stone floor, roaring and hissing, rising quickly until they scorched the ceiling. The heat was searing for just a moment, and before I could pull myself backward, I felt my eyebrows curling into charcoal. Then, just as suddenly as they had appeared, the flames vanished. I made a mental note not to ask any more questions.

"Your life is of no interest to me," he repeated, as if I were a small child who needed things explained simply and redundantly. "If you do not prove useful, you will be killed. On the other hand, I have no interest in your death, either. If you do prove useful, you will be released. That will be your reward." He studied me for a moment. "I believe you understand."

"My name is…" He looked at me, changed his mind, and continued. "My name is unimportant. As you have guessed, I come from another time, a time long ago. I was, that is, I am, the greatest magician of my era. And it is an age of great magicians.

"The world holds many secrets that science and logic will never discover. Science and logic look only to patterns. They are slaves to the rules of cause and effect. But a scientist can never discover those things that fall outside of patterns, outside the laws of cause and effect. Those things are magic.

"Eons ago it was learned that magic can only be learned by searching the foggy areas of the mind, the wild wilderness beyond logic. In fact, most magic is first stumbled upon by sheer accident. A phrase that holds power, a spell, even the luck of the stars; these things are discovered only rarely, perhaps once every hundred years or so. One cannot conduct a logical search for things that exist beyond the rule of patterns. But once learned, these secrets are carefully passed from one generation of magician to the next. No one else is told. My sect has existed since the dawn of time and has amassed such a wealth of magic as your mind cannot comprehend. And, as I said, I am the greatest of my sect. That is why I was kidnapped."

I was surprised and started to say something, but the Magician raised one eyebrow and I quickly closed my mouth again. I am nothing if not a quick learner.

"There are scientists in the future who have harnessed the vast powers of the logical world in a way that makes your current technology seem childlike. They travel through the galaxies, they travel through time... or at least they did. They'll not do that again, not for a while." He stared into space, remembering. I thought I detected some sort of satisfaction in his expression. Then he continued. "They nevertheless have incredible power.

"Like most evil men, these scientists developed a taste for this power, a taste for controlling other people. They have restricted scientific knowledge, the source of their strength, by laws and jargon until only a select few control all the knowledge. These few, of course, control the entire planet. But power is never enough. They became greedy for even more power. And somehow they learned about my sect. When they realized the power of magic, they became obsessed. They vowed to kidnap the greatest magician of all time and steal his secrets.

Armed with the power of magic – my power – in addition to the powers of science, they would be invincible. So they traveled back through time, drugged me with some sort of a gun, and took me with them. I was foolishly unprepared.

"They underestimated me, of course. I cast a Spell of Indecision on them, and they couldn't agree on what to do with me. It's sometimes called "the Committee Spell.""

The Magician was leaning against the wall now, making the torch grow brighter or more dim by moving an eyebrow, unconsciously, the way some people play with their pencil when they talk.

"While they were arguing, I stole their time-travel device and simply left. Of course, I planted the seed of "time travel fear" in each of them first. They will not follow, not for a while."

Again, the reptile smile. He was confident of his magic, I thought.

"Of my magic, yes. But not of my science. I obviously operated the time travel device improperly, and have arrived in the wrong time." He turned and stared at me coldly. "And you will help me to leave. To return to my own time. My secrets must be passed on to my apprentice. I shall not be the link that ends a chain which began in a time when science meant cooking your meat on a fire instead of eating it raw!" His voice was getting louder, I could see the anger once again in his pale face. The torch flamed up brightly, lighting the deep recesses of the dungeon. "And you shall help me return!" he shouted, then he stopped abruptly. His voice was calm and quiet when he continued, but the torch still blazed. "Or you shall die, and I will find someone else."

"But how can I…"

"The time device has an electrical control mechanism. I must learn to understand it. I have the plans, but they mean nothing to me. And, of course, I can show them to no one. I have searched your time with my mind. You are writing a book about electricity. You are camping at the lake, alone. You will not be missed. You will teach me."

I winced at the "you will not be missed" part. It seemed odd that he had found me in pretty much the same way that Mike had found

65

me. This book project was becoming a lot more bizarre than I ever expected. I noticed that he hadn't mentioned torture again.

"Only if necessary," he said, reading my mind once more. "It is usually necessary to use some sort of torture in education."

"We hardly ever use torture anymore," I said quickly, but my mind raced through all the courses I took in high school, and I wasn't so sure. "The only thing is, well, it's not exactly a standard kind of book…"

"Is it accurate?"

"Well, I don't have a degree, or anything."

"Degree?" He seemed puzzled. "I'm not familiar with the word. Is it some sort of publishing tool?"

"Well, sort of." I said. "Look, there's a lot of guys who know a lot more about this stuff than me…"

"You're it." he said flatly, and the message was clear. The discussion was over. I looked at the floor in front of me, still black and warm, and swallowed hard.

"Great!" I said. "It'll be fun."

A Medieval Electronics Lesson

"I am a very quick study," the Magician said. "You will not need to repeat yourself. How much of your book have you written?"

"Well," I said, trying to remember. Electricity seemed distant and faintly unreal in this situation. The torch light danced on the cold stone walls of the cell. "I've covered all the basic properties of electricity," I said slowly. "You know, the main characteristics that are used over and over again. I was just about to start writing about how we use those properties in circuits, and about devices that increase or decrease each characteristic."

"Fine," he said. Then he closed his eyes and tilted his head back slightly, as if concentrating, for just an instant. "You will sit there." He pointed to a small wooden table with two chairs near the wall. I would have sworn they weren't there 10 seconds ago. I got up stiffly from the damp floor and sat in one chair, he sat in the other. An oil lamp on the table began to flicker and glow, casting a moving light on both of us. "The plans that I must decipher use many strange words and symbols. As a magician, I appreciate the power of words and symbols. You will explain to me quickly the facts you have written about, for these will be freshest in your mind. Then I will release you so that you may continue to write. In a few days I will bring you back and you will explain what you have then just written. In this way your mind will be most clear, and you will waste little of my time on long and tangled explanations of simple things."

"You know," I said, "Sometimes I'm kind of a slow writer. I'll get distracted, or something else will come up. Sometimes I get writer's block and I just can't think of anything to say. It could take me months to write the next section..."

The Magician shrugged and leaned back in his chair.

"Then I will kill you. I don't have months. I must return quickly. I'm glad you have told me this before we began, so I didn't waste a lot of time. We might as well get it over with now, so I can find someone else. Nothing personal, you understand. I'll do it as painlessly as possible. Good-bye."

He closed his eyes and began to tilt his head back again.

"Wait!" I yelled. "What kind of an attitude is that! Hey, lately I've been writing real fast! Those words have been flying out of my head! Anyway, I thought you wanted to learn about electricity. What are we waiting for? Let's get started!"

He opened his eyes, a little surprised. "Are you sure?"

"You bet, no problem. One question, though. Did the plans use the word electron or anything like that?"

"Why, yes, they did! That's one of the words they use a lot."

I winced. That meant two things. First, I was going to have to explain things in terms of the electron theory. Second, it meant that the electron theory had survived into the future. That meant that the Greenie Theory probably never got off the ground, and that I would have to get a job as a piano tuner or something to support my writing habit. If I survived. But I couldn't think about that now. I took a deep breath.

"Everything is made up of atoms," I said. "Atoms have a heavy central part called a nucleus. That nucleus always has at least one proton, and sometimes it has dozens of them. A proton is a particle that has a positive charge."

"Positive charge?"

"Yeah, that's like a force field..." His face was blank. I thought for a minute. "It's like a magic spell. A proton has a positive charge, like a white magic spell surrounding it. The other thing that a nucleus can have is a neutron. Same thing as a proton except without the charge. No spell.

"Spinning around the nucleus we have electrons. Electrons are so tiny we will never be able to see one. But each one has a negative charge, like a black magic spell. Nobody understands what a charge is exactly, but we know that things are attracted to each other if they have the opposite type of charge. So electrons, with a negative charge are attracted to protons because they have a positive charge. If the electrons weren't moving so fast, they'd fall right into the proton.

"Sometimes you get a situation where there are more electrons somewhere than there are protons. The extra electrons will want to move to some spot with excess protons to equalize the charges. Protons are too bulky to move. The difference in charges between the two spots is called voltage. Voltage is measured in volts.

"When those electrons move from place to place, we refer to them as current. If many electrons are moving, we say there's a lot of current. Current is measured in amperes, or amps."

The Magician stopped me. "I'm not sure I understand the difference between current and voltage," he said.

"Voltage is the reason electrons move," I explained. "It's a percentage thing. It's the ratio between two charges. If there are 10 times as many electrons one place as another, it will have a certain voltage, whether you're talking about 10 electrons or a million electrons. Current is not a percentage or a ratio. It's supposed to be an actual traffic count. Of course, if there's lots of resistance, you won't get much current, but the voltage will still be there."

"Resistance?"

"Opposition to current flow. Some materials have electrons that are easy to dislodge from their orbital shells. They're called free electrons. If something has a lot of free electrons, it's easy for current to go through it, and we call it a good conductor. If all the electrons in a substance are bound up, rather than free, it's hard for electricity to go through it and we say it has a lot of resistance. If it has a whole lot of resistance we call it an insulator.

"Conductors that are physically small are harder for current to go through, too, so they have more resistance than larger conductors. The longer the pathway, the more the resistance. Resistance is measured in ohms."

"Got it," he said, nodding his head. "Perhaps you have not yet caught your last trout. Perhaps." It bothered me that the issue of my imminent demise was still so present in his mind. I swallowed hard, and tried to concentrate. My mouth was getting very dry.

"A circuit is a complete pathway away from a source of voltage that returns finally to that source of voltage. Electricity travels from the negatively charged side, through the circuit, to the positively charged side. An incomplete path is an open circuit and electricity won't go through it."

"Electricity and magnetism are related. Every electrical current is surrounded by a magnetic field. And every time a magnetic field moves across a conductor it causes an electrical current to flow in the conductor. When the current in a wire is increasing, the magnetic field grows. When the current is decreasing, the field shrinks. If this magnetic field moves across another wire, it will cause a current in that second wire. We call that inductance. When the magnetic field growing or shrinking around a single wire causes a voltage that opposes the change within that wire, we call it self-inductance.

"Sometimes electrons are attracted to a positively charged spot even though an insulator blocks them from completing the circuit. Electrons will tend to congregate near the insulator. The more room there is for the electrons on the conductor, the larger the effect will be. The smaller the gap in the circuit, the larger the effect. And some insulators heighten the effect. This is called capacitance. Capacitance is measured in farads.

69

"Current that changes direction rhythmically is called alternating current, or AC, to distinguish it from direct current, or DC, which moves in only one direction. Two changes in direction is called one cycle. The number of cycles per second is called the frequency."

The Magician held up his hand for me to stop.

"Enough!" he said. "That is the most boring stuff I've ever heard! My mind is very tired. As I promised, I will release you now. You will write quickly, and I will meditate on the information you have provided. Soon I will summon you here again and we shall continue. Do not forget that I am desperate, and that you cannot hide from my powers."

He paused and shook his head, then continued in an almost friendly tone, something like an editor might use, trying to be pleasant while he rejects your manuscript. "You know, Kenn, your book would probably be a lot more successful if you could think of a little more interesting way to explain electricity. You make it sound awfully dull."

I stared at my feet and nodded.

"I'll try," I said.

Series and Parallel Circuits:
Life is That Thin Place Between the Flame and the Log

The next thing I knew, I was waking up in my familiar green sleeping bag to the sound of birds circling above the lake and bacon sizzling over the campfire outside my tent. I inhaled the bacon and wood-smoke smell, opened my eyes and grinned. It had been a dream. I've been working too hard, I thought. I would spend the next couple days fishing, mellowing out, as Mike liked to say, reducing my voltage. I stepped out into the wonderful bright Utah sunlight. The weeds were coated with white frost, the sky was very blue, and the world was beautiful.

"Mike," I said, happy to see my green friend.

"You rang?" he answered.

"Boy, did I have a weird dream!"

"You always do, don't you bro'? If it's not buffaloes, it's ducks or ants or something else. What a groove! What was it this time, man? And by the way, what happened to your eyebrows?"

With a sinking feeling I ran over to the truck and looked at my face in the rear-view mirror. My eyebrows were nearly gone, and the few little hairs remaining were no more than threads of black carbon. I went back to the campfire and told Mike about the dream.

"Bummer, man. A bad trip. A real downer."

I think he was expressing sympathy.

"You got to dig this, man," he continued. "I'm new here. Greenies are no strangers to weirdness, but this guy gives even me the creeps. Maybe there's some good explanation, but I don't know what it is. Mosquitoes didn't burn off your eyebrows."

Indeed they did not, I thought. But a master magician from the distant past, kidnapped into the future who mistakenly escaped into 20th century Utah and wanted to be tutored in basic electricity? Almost easier to believe in electrons.

"Look," said Mike. "Maybe you did it with your own mind, somehow. Maybe you walked in your sleep and got too close to the embers from last night's campfire. Whatever. But until we figure it out, I think you gotta assume the dude's for real. You want to write the book anyway, and I want to get back to my chick. I think the hot program is just to move forward, keep writing and see what happens."

"I guess you're right."

"Right on! By now we're supposed to be talking about series circuits and parallel circuits. Let's go for it."

"Okay," I said, looking around me nervously. The familiar lake, trees, and rocks were no longer so comforting to me. The morning was chilly, and I realized that summer had slipped away and the leaves were changing color.

"A series circuit is a road that never forks, that has no side streets. No choices to make. You get headed down that street and it's the only street in town. You go past a tree, a hamburger joint, six houses and a used car lot. Then you're back where you started. Got that?"

"What?" I answered.

"Concentrate, man," he said. "A series circuit is one where the Greenies have no choices. They go down the road, past each landmark in order until they complete the loop and return to the voltage source."

"Okay" I said, "That's easy enough."

"A parallel circuit is just a little different. In a parallel circuit there is a fork in the road. A choice those Greenies have to make. You're boogying down the road, and it's a series circuit so far. You go past the tree, the hamburger joint, six houses and a used car lot. Then the road forks. To the left is cornfields. To the right is a whole row of Chinese restaurants. Sooner or later those two roads will join up again, but for now you've got to choose.

"Some Greenies are going to head down one road and some down the other. When they get to the party, they'll all be able to talk about the tree, the hamburger joint, the six houses and the used car lot. The series part of the circuit. But some of them will smell like egg roll, and the rest will have corn silk in their teeth. They all wound up at the same party. They took different but parallel routes. Part of the time they were in series and part of the time they were in parallel.

That made sense. In a series circuit all the electricity goes through each part of the circuit in the same order. In a parallel circuit electricity takes one or more alternate paths to reach the same destination. Some of the electricity goes down one path and some down another.

"What if one path has more resistance?" I asked.

"Good point. If you come to a fork in the road and one way looks rocky, most of the Greenies will head down the easy path. But some will take the hard route, the path of most resistance. Guys in four-wheel drive vehicles, for example, seem to choose the hardest path. The more difference there is in resistance between the two, the greater the difference will be in current.

"Another neat thing about resistance in parallel circuits: When you add an alternate route, no matter how much resistance it has, it reduces the over-all resistance in the circuit."

"Whoa!" I said. "You add resistance to a parallel circuit and it reduces over all resistance? We're going to lose a lot of readers right there."

Mike laughed, then continued patiently.

72

"A footbridge over a canyon has a lot more resistance than the paved highway that led up to it. Adding a second footbridge, even though it also has a lot of resistance, makes it twice as easy to get across. Adding an alternate route always makes it easier to get somewhere, no matter how much resistance it has. It will alleviate some amount of traffic problems."

"If you build twenty foot bridges across that canyon there'd be a lot less of a traffic jam. Any bridge has some resistance of course, so you're adding parallel paths of resistance. But the over all effect is less resistance."

"I wonder when he's going to come and get me again," I said. Mike just shook his head.

"Cut me some slack, will you bro'?" he said in disgust. "I've got a stake in this too, you know. You get fried and I'll be looking for work as the green man in the circus. Don't let your mind boggle on you. Get down, get funky. We got work to do. You go back over series and parallel circuits until you got it down cold. I suspect old torch-fingers will be a mite peeved if you give him bum dope and he breaks the time-travel machine. Think about it. Stuck in Utah forever and you to blame? Not a nice thought."

I could see his point, and went to work.

Making Electricity

We can't actually make electricity any more than we can make peace. It's just a phrase. We convert some other form of energy, like heat, or motion or chemical energy into electrical energy. Actually we use them to create voltage and let nature take its course. We do this because electricity is versatile, clean, storable and we can transport it long distances relatively easily. Waterfalls and nuclear power plants are not portable.

We already know that when a magnetic field moves past a conductor it creates an electrical current. This principle is responsible for the vast majority of the electricity that is created on planet Earth. Typically the conductor is a very long wire coiled many times. Picture a long wire wrapped around a round oatmeal box until it completely covers the box several layers thick. The wire was covered with a thin coat of enamel before this happened, so it's insulated from itself. If you put a magnet inside this oatmeal box and spin it, the lines of magnetic force will cut across that wire again and again. The energy you use to spin the magnet will be converted to electricity in the wire. The faster you spin, the more voltage you create. The stronger the magnet, the more voltage. You may help the permanent magnet by adding an electromagnet that uses some of the current we are producing. The more current we produce, the stronger the electromagnet, which allows us to create even more current.

If this device uses only a permanent magnet, it's called a "magneto." The little device on bicycles that lights the headlight is a magneto, and so is the device that provides electricity to your lawn mower's spark plug. When the lawn mower is running, the gasoline engine turns the blade (and the magneto), and the magneto provides that little bit of electricity for the spark plug. Until the engine takes over, many lawn mowers require their owner to pull a cord, which turns the engine and the magneto, to provide those first couple of sparks.

If the device uses an electromagnet, and is set up to produce DC, it's called a "generator." The earliest cars used generators.

If a generator is set up to produce AC, it's called an "alternator." Your car probably has an alternator to keep the battery charged and to power your lights, horn and spark plugs. A lot of people use the word generator when they mean alternator. In most situations it doesn't matter ("don't drop the generator on your foot, dear," for example). If you want to make plans based on what kind of current you can expect out of the thing, it becomes more critical. Generators produce DC, alternators produce AC.

The part of a generator or alternator that spins is called the "rotor." The part that is stationary is called the "stator." I only mention it because I sense you are hungry for some more jargon. If you're still not satisfied, the electromagnet may be on either the stator or the rotor. The electromagnet itself is called the "field" and the coil of wire you're trying to produce electricity within is called the "armature." Please don't remember these words. People will think you're showing off.

74

As an alternator (or generator) spins, lines of magnetic force cross a wire and create a current within it. You can use anything you want to spin the thing. There are small generators with hand cranks. World War I soldiers powered their field radios with hand-crank generators. If you have a stream, you could use a water wheel to turn your alternator. If you dam the stream, you can let water fall from the top of the dam, down hundreds of feet to the bottom, let it flash through a turbine, and connect the turbine to your rotor. You could let your windmill turn it. You can let a fan belt in your car turn it. If you happen to have a lot of steam laying around, you can contain it in a boiler and let it escape through a turbine to turn your alternator. You say you have no steam? Heat some water. Burn coal, natural gas, wood, newspapers, or trash to heat your water. That's what the power companies do. Concentrate sunlight with mirrors onto your boiler and you'll get steam. If you are lucky enough to have a geyser in your back yard, you can hook up directly to this natural source of steam. And, of course, nuclear reactions produce a lot of heat. Nuclear power plants use this heat to create steam to turn turbines to spin the magnet in the oatmeal box and produce electricity. That's why we have nuclear reactors. For the heat.

The next most common method of stirring Greenies to action is by using chemicals. If you fill an empty soup can with an acid (like vinegar or lime juice, for example), and then float a piece of carbon (coal, charcoal, graphite, etc) in the center of that acid, you have done it. The chemical will react with the metal of the can and the carbon and produce a voltage. Provide an easy path between the carbon and the can (easier than swimming through the acid) and current will flow. The container can be made of almost any type of metal. Instead of carbon, you could have used almost any metal that was different than the can. You could have used any acid, or you could have used a alkaline (opposite of acid) like ammonia or lye. Shoot, you could have used a cola drink. Of course, some combinations work better than others.

If you have one of these cans, it's called a "cell." Add some stuff to soak up your acid and keep it from oozing out all over your flashlight and it's a "dry cell." Several cells together are called a battery. Your car probably has six "wet cells" made of lead plates separated by acid, each one producing two volts, organized into one neat box and sold as a 12-volt battery.

The dry cell in your flashlight is a primary cell. The chemical action creates a voltage, but sooner or later the materials will be exhausted and you'll have to throw it away. Your car battery is made of secondary cells; if you add electricity you can reverse the chemical process and "re-charge" it over and over again. A battery of secondary cells is often called a storage battery.

Batteries have the advantage of portability, convenience and that they can store energy to be used as needed. People who employ windmills to turn their generators usually use the power they produce to re-charge their storage batteries. It seems that the wind is never blowing when your favorite TV show comes on.

The other four methods of producing electricity are minor in comparison with magnetism and chemicals. If you press two different kinds of metal together and heat them, they will produce electricity. This is used in electronic thermometers and other heat-detection devices, like the safety switch on your furnace. If no electricity is coming from the "thermocouple," your furnace turns off the gas to itself, because it knows that the pilot light has expired. Thermocouples, or "bimetallic strips," are not very efficient. As evidence of symmetry in the universe, if you run current through a bimetallic strip, it will get cold. This nifty feature has not yet been utilized much, but some portable coolers employ the principle.

If you squeeze certain crystals, they will produce a tiny current. This is called the "piezoelectric effect." As more evidence of symmetry, if you run some current through that same crystal, it will expand. This has some neat applications.

Sunlight shining on certain materials causes a small amount of electricity. Many people hope that this phenomenon can be refined so that solar-produced electricity replaces some of the other methods. So far it's too expensive to be competitive.

Friction can create electricity, as we already discussed, but it's static electricity. This is primarily used to screw up computers and zap cat noses, although it is also used in some copying machines and FAX machines.

Mike Complains About My Writing

"Boring, boring, boring! Gag me with a spoon!"

I could tell Mike was not impressed with my chapter on making electricity.

"But I got in a heck of a bunch of jargon," I said, perhaps a bit defensively. "Even a couple of words no one will ever use, just like the real books do. Plus, I covered all the important ways that electricity is produced."

"But who cares, man? There was not one Greenie, not one buffalo, no ducks, no ants, no little sports cars, no motorboats. You're letting old torch-fingers get to you. You're losing all your style. No offense, but that chapter sucks eggs. Could've been a school book."

"I didn't think it was that bad," I sniffed.

Mike just grunted.

"Look," I said. "There's six ways to produce electricity. Two ways are used almost all the time. Either we move a magnetic field near a wire, or we use chemicals. I could write a whole book about the different designs of generators, and the chemical reactions in batteries if you want to really understand the word 'boring.' The basic concept is so easy, I don't think we need any little picture stories. These are intelligent readers we've got here."

"No beer, no party, no rock 'n roll." Mike was pouting.

"I thought I got in the phrase 'piezoelectric effect' rather smoothly," I said. "You know, where a crystal produces electricity when you subject it to pressure. And how about 'bimetallic strip?' Two different metals pressed together that produce electricity when you heat them. We mentioned static electricity produced by friction. And light shining on solar cells. If these readers had to take a test right now on the six ways to produce electricity, and which two are most important, they'd ace it. Simple, concise, easy to understand. Not too many details, then move on. It's the way I run my life."

"No surfing, no Greenie girls. Like a textbook."

"I'll try to do better."

The Intergalactic Steam Circus

You and I have the most interesting jobs in the universe: We run the Intergalactic Steam Circus, a most outrageous and bizarre affair. Travelling in wildly colorful space clippers, we sail from planet to planet in a huge parade, landing just outside the major population centers, setting up our magnificent and gaudy tents, and selling the people our magic of noise, confusion, bright lights, and trickery. There are, of course, beautiful young women strutting like cats in scanty sequined outfits, and handsome young men with tanned and muscular bodies, their shirts open to the waist. But that's not what draws the crowds, day after day, planet after planet. They come to see the machinery.

That's right, folks. Step right up! See the machine that pumps water! See the machine that grinds corn! Ride around the big tent in our Intergalactic Circus Train! A thousand delights, ladies and gentlemen, a thousand delights, and every single one of them is powered by that Mystical Demon, that Genie in a Bottle, that Marvel of the Universe! You know it's true, ladies and gentlemen! A thousand delights, all powered by steam!

Steam?

You bet! Okay, so the show isn't a big hit on the more advanced planets. But give me a medieval mentality and I'll sell all the cotton candy and popcorn you can make. Steam power revolutionized industry, yet it's pretty much a one-trick pony. You heat water, it boils away into steam. If you confine the steam and keep heating it, it tries to expand, building up pressure. Divert that pressure into a cylinder and it will push a piston. Aim it at a fan or turbine to spin them. Let it escape through pipe-organ pipes and it will wake up your neighborhood in a big hurry. (That's what a calliope is, by the way: a pipe organ that uses steam. You can bet our circus has the biggest calliope in the Milky Way.) Steam expands. That's all it's good for. As it expands it pushes things out of its way.

Most older steam engines used steam to push a piston back and forth inside a cylinder. The wonderful inventiveness of man took advantage of this simple device to build our whole circus full of marvels. By attaching a weight to one end of the piston we made the steam hammer that put John Henry out of business. By hooking the equivalent of a bicycle pump to the piston we created a water pump that saved the lives of thousands of miners. By hooking a crank-shaft to the piston we changed the back and forth motion of the piston into circular motion that could power a locomotive or car, or grinder, or cotton gin, or power saw, or tractor.

The modern world, and our beautiful circus, was all made possible because steam expands when you heat it. That's all it does. Yet it powered a thousand devices, each one doing something different. The same principle that makes your tea kettle whistle also made locomotives pull redwood trees from California over the Rocky Mountains and made cotton gins pull the seeds out of cotton bolls.

Electricity is not a one-trick pony. It's a three-trick pony. All the stereo systems, golf carts, electric guitars, arc welders and digital watches of the world are possible because of these three tricks. And you already know two of them:

When electricity goes through a conductor it creates a magnetic field; and when electricity passes through resistance, some of the electrical energy is converted to heat.

The third one is just as simple: Some materials glow when Greenies run into them.

Phosphorus is one of these materials. We coat the front of TV picture tubes with phosphorus, or something like it. Your set is designed to continually slam Little Greenies into the front of the picture tube just to make that stuff glow. Neon gas is another example. Fill a tube with neon gas, run some electricity through it, and the gas will glow. Bingo! Neon lights.

The "phosphorescent effect" is neat, but we couldn't build a whole circus around it. Our two "biggies," the stars of center stage, the two ponies that pay the mortgage on our circus equipment, are our two old friends, heat and magnetism.

You know that every time electricity travels through a conductor it causes some heat. This is because everything has at least a little resistance. Conductors that have a lot of resistance will produce more heat. If you put some high-resistance wire in your circuit it will get especially hot. A section of high resistance material added to a circuit on purpose just so it can produce heat is called a "heating element."

We all love to look inside the toaster while it's working. Those little wires glowing red inside it are heating elements. They're made of a high resistance wire. The large wires in an electric stove that glow red-hot and broil your steaks are the heating elements. There is a heating element encased in waterproof plastic under your waterbed mattress that keeps you toasty at night. Electric coffeepots have a heating element. Clothes dryers have a heating element. If they ever invent electric cats, they will have a heating element in them too, so they can keep your lap warm.

Life would be a lot different if Greenies didn't get angry and hot when forced to move through resistance. If an electrical device is supposed to produce heat, there's probably a high-resistance heating element lurking in it somewhere.

Life would also be a lot different if every electrical current wasn't surrounded by magnetism. Most of the electrical devices that *move* in one way or another use an electromagnet to do the moving. Think about that; if an electrical device is moving, an electromagnet is probably at work. Magnetism is the only practical way to get much physical motion out of electricity. Electric motors use electromagnets, and electric motors are what power golf carts, refrigerators, water pumps, electric train sets, escalators, sirens, power windows, air conditioners and conveyor belts. If it turns or spins, there is probably an electric motor turning it, working because of magnetism. Stereo speakers use electromagnets to create sound. Aquarium pumps use electromagnets to make that terrible buzzing sound, and, if you're lucky, to make some bubbles for your guppies. Televisions use electromagnets to control the picture.

Heat and magnetism are the main links between the world of the Greenie and the world of humans. If not for them, we would probably still be trying to develop steam-powered computers.

How can this be, you ask? How can all the variety of electrical devices have, at their heart, at that final stage, no more than this? A couple of examples will show you.

The electric motor is a device of wonderful simplicity. Imagine a merry-go-round at the circus, with iron horses to ride on. Showman that I am, I will place an unbelievably beautiful young woman on each horse, dressed in some dazzling outfit, smiling and waving to the crowd. They will have absolutely no effect on the analogy; I just wanted to have them there.

Clowns stand around the merry-go-round at even intervals, each of them holding a powerful electromagnet. At our signal, one clown turns on his electromagnet. Slowly but surely the magnet pulls the nearest iron horse toward him. When it gets close, he turns off his magnet. Of course, the whole merry-go-round is turning now, very slowly. It will take a few seconds for it to coast to a stop. Before that can happen, we signal the second clown, he turns on his electromagnet and pulls an iron horse toward him.

You see that if we can get our clowns organized to turn their magnets on and off at just the right times, that merry-go-round will keep turning, and, as its inertia is overcome, it will go faster and faster. That is exactly how an electric motor works. Electromagnets, in a circle, surrounding a rotor, that we turn on and off systematically.

A music speaker uses an electromagnet in a similar way. A thin piece of iron is placed close to the electromagnet. As we increase the current, the magnet will pull the metal toward it. When we decrease the current, the magnet will become weaker and the metal will spring back toward its original position. Each variation in current will cause that thin metal to move. If it is moving fast enough, we will hear a hum, as the vibrating metal makes the air around it vibrate. We can fasten the metal to some cardboard or plastic, giving it a larger surface area and it will move more air. If we control the current very precisely, we can make the magnet change so quickly and in such elaborate and subtle ways that the strip of metal will sound like a symphony orchestra, or even Chuck Berry.

There is a limit to the speed that a magnet can change, especially if you have enhanced your electromagnet by putting an iron core inside it. (Did you notice how deftly I slipped the term "core" into the conversation? The "core" is whatever you fill a coil with. There are air cores and iron cores and oatmeal box cores. Good electromagnets usually have an iron core.) A magnet's resistance to change is called "hysteresis," which is one of my personal favorites, as far as jargon is concerned. I can easily picture a hysterical magnet, pouting that it must change strength or polarity (north to south & vice versa). As you increase the speed of change in your speaker, you're fighting the hysteresis of the electromagnet. As you approach 20,000 cycles your magnet can't cope any more; it breaks down and cries little magnetic tears, and the high violin passages sound distorted.

Except for a few wonderful but less common tricks, the final product of all electrical devices involves either magnetism, heat, or phosphorescence. The same human creativity that manipulated the simple expansion of steam into an entire industrial revolution has embraced these three and used them as the building blocks for radio, satellite TV, computers, and radial arm saws.

And they all work because Greenies like to party.

The Light Bulb

"Poor old Thomas Alva," said the man in the gray tweed coat, shaking his head sadly. "He's doing it again."

Six very proper men leaned on the polished oak bar, nodding their heads in agreement as they drank their beers. The tavern was small and dark; it smelled of leather and pipe smoke. The other customers, all men, sat in small groups around tables talking quietly. From the next room came the occasional louder sound of pool balls, laughter and cursing, and the coarser smell of cigars. The group at the bar looked serious.

"That's too bad," the bartender replied, but his grin told what he really thought. He owned this place, and these were his regular customers. Whenever old Thomas Alva "went eccentric," as he put it, this group of friends got nervous and wound up buying a lot of beer. Thomas did some pretty odd things.

"It's worse this time," one of them said, motioning at the bartender to set up another round. "He's talking about little Greenies." Nobody laughed. They were all concerned about their strange friend, and wondered how long they could keep his flights into Never-Never Land a secret.

"He's fooling around with little bitty heating elements, too," another one whispered, looking over his shoulder as if to make sure no one else was listening.

"That's a new one."

"I mean *tiny* little bitty heating elements. Smaller than a wire. He calls them filaments."

"But what will he use them for?"

"That's just the point! There is no use for them!"

Everyone shook their heads in wonder and drank down their beers. It's going to be a good night, the bartender thought.

"It gets worse," the first one said.

"No!" the bartender said, wiping a glass with a towel, barely able to conceal his glee.

"Yes! He's trying all these different things as heating elements, or filaments as he says. Weird things. He used hair from a horse's tail. He used cotton string. Next thing you know he'll be using bat wings and toad's eyes. It's just not healthy! If anybody ever found out…"

"Quiet! Here he comes!" They all turned to see a stocky man in a rumpled coat approaching them through the crowded bar. His eyes were wide open, his face was red. There was an air of tremendous excitement about him.

"Bamboo! Bamboo!" he shouted at them. It sounded like he was imitating some exotic bird. "Bamboo!" he shouted once again, and the other customers seemed to edge away from him.

"Quiet, Tom, it's all right. Here, have a beer."

He drained it in a gulp.

"Bamboo!" he repeated, more quietly this time, then he opened one hand, as if to show them a priceless diamond. He held a sliver of charcoal. The bartender began to whistle merrily.

"Electrical friction!" Thomas said. "It heated up the bamboo! Fried it to a crisp!"

"Right, Tom. How about another beer? It's going to be just fine."

"Don't you see? I used a tiny piece of bamboo as a heating element. The bamboo got hot, so hot it glowed! It was beautiful. Like…

83

like… like a chair burning… only smaller, of course. We're very close now. It only lasted a few seconds, but…" He paused, his eyes staring into the distance. His friends looked in the direction he was staring, but he had gone to a place where they could not follow. Then his face brightened.

"Oxygen! Of course! If I remove the oxygen from around the bamboo, it will still get so hot it glows, but it won't burn up! Can't burn up without oxygen! Don't you see? If I use a tiny heating element…did I tell you I call them filaments? Right, I remember now… if I heat this filament in, say, a jar until it glows, it will make a light. If there's no oxygen in the jar, it will glow for a long time. You could light up a whole aquarium that way! I think I'll call them "light jars." Everyone who has an aquarium will want one! We'll be rich!"

He lifted his face to stare at the ceiling, looking for a moment like a coyote about to howl "bamboo!" again. His friends held their breath. Then, without another word, he turned and left the bar. His friends exhaled in unison and stared after him, their mouths hanging open.

"Another round?" the bartender asked cheerily. They all nodded.

"Poor old Thomas Alva," they said as they reached for their beers.

Components:
Symbols, Schematics and "No Fishing" Signs

If you post a lot of "No Fishing" signs around your property, people are going to believe that you are guarding some fabulous fishing spot. Otherwise, why would you put up the signs? They will believe you are a greedy, self-centered person who deserves to be trespassed against, and your signs will go unheeded. Nay, those signs will act as beacons to the swarming fishermen who will descend, like moths, upon your farm.

On the other hand a few signs saying "Welcome to the Annual Internal Revenue Service Convention; Public Invited" will probably ensure that you can keep your fish all to yourself.

The title of this chapter is like that. I just wanted to remind you how effective jargon can be at weeding out less dedicated readers.

There will not be a test. If you are reading this book because you hope to one day do complicated stuff inside electrical equipment, and get paid for it, then you're going to want to understand how to read electrical diagrams and figure exact specifications. In that case, great, read every word of every following chapter, and take careful notes as you have been doing all along.

But if you are only mildly curious about electricity, even now, do not despair. There is much fun yet ahead. If you see an occasional formula or diagram that makes you nervous, simply close your eyes and turn a page or two, just like real scientists do. You won't miss a thing. For those of you who have come this far, and who still have your fishing poles, grab your bait and pick a spot in the shade.

"Components" is a fancy word that means "little electrical parts." All those weird looking, multi-colored, bug-sized things lurking deep inside your television set are components. There are only a dozen or so varieties, but each type can be made in many shapes, sizes and colors. This is done to confuse people. A battery is a component. A light bulb is a component. Components are the things we put together in different ways to manipulate our Greenies.

Now we're going to "up the ante" in the jargon game – turn pro, as it were. Not only will we give each little component its own name, we're going to give it a "symbol," a little picture that can represent it wordlessly in diagrams. Electrical symbols are like the notes on paper that musicians use to write music. They are nearly identical around the world, a universal language that all electronics experts recognize. Since you and I want people to think we're experts, we ought to learn them, too.

Perhaps the most common component of all is wire. A simple conductor, very little resistance. The symbol for wire is a straight line. Notice that I said a straight line. Neither you nor I have ever seen a straight wire, but that's what you draw when you make a schematic. Nice straight lines, that usually only make 90-degree turns. A straight line is also the symbol for any good conductor besides wire. Aluminum foil conducts electricity just as well as a wire does. In your schematic they'll look just the same.

Symbol for a conductor: ████████████████

85

When two conductors are electrically connected, there may be a black dot at their intersection:

Sometimes two lines will have to cross each other because a drawing only has two dimensions and wires can loop over and under each other. In some diagrams, if there's no black dot, the two conductors are independent, and it's just coincidence that the lines cross. This was important when people used pencils to draw diagrams by hand on paper. Now, it depends on your computer program. Most programs don't fool with black dots, so we won't either. To avoid confusion, some diagrams will have a little arc in one line if the two conductors are not connected electrically:

It doesn't matter if the lines are dark or light, or big or small, crude or fancy. I'll try to keep mine crude and not uniform, to prepare you for the real world, and certainly not because I can't figure out the program that draws them. A battery of cells has a series of positive and negative surfaces. The symbol for a battery reminds you of this:

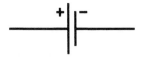

Every time you see that symbol, whether you're in Topeka or Zurich, someone has just told you there's a battery in a circuit.

Remember switches? Switches are like gates in a fence that interrupt an ant's journey around the pig pen. The symbol for a switch makes sense in that context:

You can see that it looks like a gate which is open. It's easy to picture it swinging closed and completing the circuit. If you drew it that way, however, it would look like two dots on a line, and would be easy to overlook. Switches are usually pictured open, but we all know that sometimes they will be closed.

One more example. A light bulb is a jar with no oxygen and a tiny heating element that gets so hot it glows. Bamboo has been largely replaced by tungsten as the material for the filament. The symbol for a light bulb is:

When you draw a picture of a circuit using these symbols, you call the picture a "schematic diagram," or simply a "schematic." Literally translated, that means a "picture of the scheme," and that's usually pretty accurate. You can buy a schematic diagram of your television set and use it as a road map to locate parts and help figure out which one just quit on you. You can buy a schematic diagram of the latest special effect for your electric guitar, buy the components, and use the schematic as a blue-print to build it. You can save your band a lot of money by doing that.

If you like jargon, you'll fall in love with schematic diagrams. Think of it: jargon without words! There's a certain intellectual beauty to that. Like all truly great jargon, schematic diagrams are wonderful shorthand, conveying huge amounts of information quickly and easily, while imposing a glorious obstacle to the un-initiated. With the possible exceptions of Latin, algebra, and the federal budget, jargon-wise, this is It. The big time.

We can put all of our symbols together into a schematic diagram:

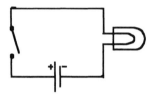

This is a perfectly good circuit containing a battery, some wire, a switch and a light bulb. Close the switch and your light will come on. In fact, this is the exact schematic diagram for a flashlight, even though some flashlights use their metal case as a conductor instead of a wire. Electrically, there's no difference. You have begun to read schematics.

The Importance of Being Norwegian

It is a not-well-known fact that every single person who has contributed to the science of electronics has been Norwegian. The Norwegians are a very private people, even shy, and they simply don't seek out the fame they deserve in many arenas. Here's an example: Expert jargonists, they concealed the delicacy of their favorite seafood from the world by naming it "lutefisk." To create lutefisk, you dry heavily salted dead codfish in slabs and stack their hideous mummified bodies like firewood on the back porch. When that starts to sound tempting, you lug a carcass inside, soak it in lye until it's leathery, then boil it all day in several changes of clear water. Lutefisk is a food you may never have requested in a fine restaurant, simply because you never heard of it. My father claims it tastes just like lobster. Luckily, you don't need to eat lutefisk to learn electronics.

In a similar way, these shy folk have avoided all the acclaim that is due their scientific community by adopting less Norwegian-sounding names. By adopting pseudonyms like "Einstein," "Marconi," "Faraday," and "Kirschoff," Norwegian scientists have managed to keep their homeland pure of celebrity-seekers and cheap newspapers. I feel the time has come to correct their misplaced modesty and set the record straight. I am, after all, half Norwegian myself. I hope that someday they'll understand and realize I've done the right thing.

Anyway, I have eaten lutefisk. They owe me something.

Interestingly enough, the one exception to their caution has been the word "schematic." This is an old Norwegian term which refers to the plans that young Norwegian boys used for sneaking out of the house at night to visit the girls who cared for goats in the high pastures during the summer:

"Vot's de schematic, Thormod?"

"Vell, I'll say I'm going to bed, sure, and den ven de ol' volks go to sleep, vee vill slip out de vindow."

"Ya, sure, dat's a good schematic."

"Tanks a lot."

Now, of course, a schematic means a diagram of an electrical circuit.

A New Component: The Resistor

Suppose you wake up in the middle of the night with the urge to add some resistance to a circuit. Maybe your flashlight is just too darn bright. You figure that if you could only reduce the current going through that little light bulb you could tone it down a bit, perhaps create a more romantic mood. You remember that adding resistance to a circuit will reduce the current, but how in the world can you do that?

Those of you who have learned by now that the best part of most of my chapters is their titles will be able to answer that question easily.: You add a resistor.

Resistors are little components that each have a very specific amount of resistance. If you want to add 10 ohms of resistance, put a 10 ohm resistor into the circuit. If you want to add 10,000 or a million ohms, we have resistors that can do that for you. No problem.

There are three reasons something can have a lot of resistance.

It can be made of a material that is naturally high in resistance; many resistors are nothing more than bits of carbon mounted in a protective case. Carbon has quite a bit of resistance and it's cheap.

Conductors that are physically small (the footbridge principle) have a lot of resistance. Foil that is so thin it is really just a microscopic film of metal mounted on an insulator will act as a resistor, and, in fact, will be called a "metal film resistor."

Finally, a very long pathway will have more resistance than a short one. Adding a couple of miles of wire to your circuit would work, but it isn't done. Too expensive, too cumbersome. Perhaps because it's the one method seldom used, the symbol for a resistor represents an extra long pathway added to a circuit:

So, now we can dim our flashlight and prove that we did by drawing a schematic:

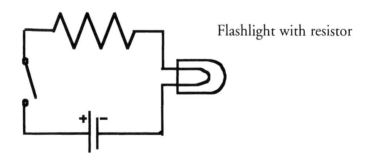

Flashlight with resistor

Ohm: His Name, His Law, His Mantra

Well, his name was really Lars Thorvillson, but like most Norwegian scientists he disguised himself by adopting the name George Simon Ohm.

Lars, I mean, Mr. Ohm, knew what you and I know: The amount of current in a circuit is affected by both the voltage and the resistance.

His special contribution was that he realized there was a very specific, measurable relationship between the three. By adopting arbitrary sizes for the units he formalized both the units and the relationship.

Ohm said, "Let's assume one unit of voltage can push one unit of current through one unit of resistance, and see what happens." As you know, a unit of voltage is known as one volt. A unit of current is one amp. At that point, apparently, his modesty ran out of juice and he named a unit of resistance one "ohm." In a further moment of weakness, he named the relationship he had discovered "Ohm's Law," and it's still called that. Don't believe your teachers when they tell you that these names were adopted much later to honor old George Simon. I think he did it himself, and the real lesson, the real Ohm's Law is this: If you want a bridge or park to be named after you, just do it. Who knows, maybe it'll stick.

In a nutshell, the electrical version of Ohm's Law goes like this: One volt will push one amp of current through one ohm of resistance. If you change one, they'll all change.

I believe that when he wrote the thing down he was using Norwegian words, however. He abbreviated voltage with a capital "E", ampere with a capital "I" and ohm with an "R". Either that or he was a lot more advanced as a jargonist than he is usually given credit for. If you change any of the variables, you can figure out how it affects the others by this nifty formula:

$$Voltage = (Current)(Resistance)$$

In the abbreviated Norwegian form, which is still used, it looks like this:

$$E = IR$$

That means, voltage (E) equals the current (I) times the resistance (R). If we know there's 10 amps of current going through 10 ohms of resistance, we can figure there's 100 volts pushing (or pulling) the Greenies.

If we see five amps of current going through six ohms of resistance, like this:

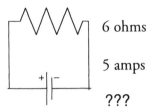

6 ohms

5 amps

???

then we know that the battery is a 30-volt battery. See how neat that works? Current times resistance equals voltage. And you can do more.

Suppose we buy a 10-volt battery and we connect it to a five-ohm resistor. We are curious about how much current is flowing. Those of you who understood simple junior high school math (which I did not) will quickly see that the formula can be rearranged to provide that information. Current equals voltage divided by resistance. The mutated formula looks like this:

$$I=E/R$$

If it's been a while since you've done any math without a calculator, remember that two symbols next to each other (Like "IR") means multiply them (I times R). When one is above the other or separated by a slash (E/R) it means divide the top one by the bottom one (E divided by R). The line separating the two means "divided by." To find the current in our example, we replace the letters in the formula with the values that we know:

$$I=10/5$$

then do the math. Ten divided by five equals two. Two amps of current are flowing through our little circuit.

We can also rearrange the formula to determine resistance if we know the other two factors. Simply divide the voltage by the current:

$$R=E/I$$

In this circuit:

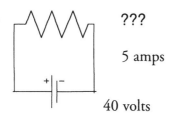

???

5 amps

40 volts

voltage (40) divided by current (5) equals resistance. Forty divided by five equals eight. That's an 8-ohm resistor.

Ohm's Law, simple as it is, gave me fits. In the first place, what sense do the abbreviations make? I am able to remember that "E" stands for voltage because it might stand for "enthusiasm" which is a lot like need-to-party. "R" is obviously resistance. That leaves "I" for current, which I found tough. I tried to remember that current is the actual number of Greenies moving through a wire, and pictured those little green guys, in little green sports cars yelling, "I am current! I am current." It didn't work. Finally I settled for "E" means enthusiasm, which means voltage. "R" means resistance. And the only one left is "I" so that must be current.

Then I couldn't remember when to multiply and when to divide, and which letter goes on top. I decided to settle for remembering the basic formula:

$$E = IR$$

which is just multiplication. The formula starts with enthusiasm, (voltage) so I decided to keep track of "E" in the other two versions. Turns out it's always on top. Trying to determine the current? Use this:

$$I = E/R$$

Trying to determine the resistance? Use this:

$$R = E/I$$

Lars could have made it easier, one could argue, but then it wouldn't have been jargon, it wouldn't have been electronics, it wouldn't have been nearly as much fun. Ohm's Law is worth a little effort. There's really nothing as impressive as slipping little formulas into an otherwise ordinary conversation.

There are probably three or four million Americans who understand Ohm's Law as well as you do right now; who knows, you may run into one of them. Maybe you'll even fall in love with one of them. At least you won't be embarrassed if they cautiously bring it up. If that many people can handle it, you can too.

On the other hand, three or four million people represent less than two per cent of the American population. You have joined a very exclusive club.

The Rest of the Story

The year is 1827. Steam locomotives have not yet been invented, there are no railroads. People wait for stagecoaches in the lobbies of hotels. The stagecoach is seldom on time, luggage is routinely misplaced, the clerks are often rude, and occasionally a band of thieves hijacks a coach. It is a primitive, uncivilized time. Not at all like today.

We are somewhere in Europe, in a hotel lobby bustling with travelers waiting for their stagecoaches. Many have bags, some sleep fitfully in chairs, a few talk in quiet groups. Wherever you look, people walk in an unending procession, glancing at their pocket watches, anxious and preoccupied. In one corner of the huge room an oddly dressed man is avoiding a middle-aged Norwegian woman.

"Lars! Is that you? Lars Thorvillson!" The heavyset woman was persistent.

"You must be confused, ma'am," he replied. His tone was pleasant, but he was obviously nervous. "My name is Ohm. George Simon Ohm."

"Come on, Lars, I know it's you! I haven't seen you since the big picnic in Stavanger. What are you doing so far from home? And why are you dressed like that?" The man was dressed in a white flowing robe and his hair was all shaved except for one long pony tail.

"You are mistaken, madam. My name is George, not Lars. But here, let me give you a flower." He handed her a long-stemmed iris that was a beautiful, deep blue color.

"Why, thank you Lars, I mean, George, or whatever you call yourself these days."

"The flower is my gift to you, and I hope it brightens your day," he said in a calm, practiced voice. As she took the flower and admired it, he continued. "I am working to bring peace and harmony to the world. That is my mission in life. The iris flower symbolizes that. If you would also like to see peace and harmony in the world, any contribution you can make would be appreciated."

The woman looked surprised by his request for money, and a bit flustered. Of course she wanted peace and harmony in the world. And, after all, she had taken the flower. She felt a little trapped and oddly guilty as she found some money in her bag and gave it to him.

"Have a nice day," he said, as she hurried away from him. He turned to a young man a few feet away who had been watching the whole thing.

"See," he said. "That's how it's done. You give 'em the iris, then make your pitch. Never fails."

"It looks easy," the young man admitted. Like George, he wore a robe and had a nearly shaved head. "And then, at the end of the day, I give you the money, right?"

"Exactly. You give me the money and all the boxes of iris flowers you haven't sold, I mean, given away. I know you're an honest fellow, but there may be others who are not so honest. I've been doing this so long I know exactly how much money you should receive for each box of irises. I keep track of how many people you've contacted by how many irises you've given away."

"That's pretty neat!" The young man was impressed.

"Thank you. With peace-workers in every stagecoach station in Europe and America, my bookkeeping would be a nightmare without systems."

"And what do I get for doing this?"

"Ah, you're the lucky one. You get the satisfaction of helping to bring peace and harmony to the world! You are molding a new world, my son, a global family, an era of tranquility and unity with all living things. Plus you get a bowl of rice for lunch, and you get to keep the sandals."

"Wow!" The young man could hardly wait to bring peace and harmony to the world. "But why do we have to be stuck back in this corner?"

"It's a new regulation. They won't let us out into the main part of the lobby. They think we annoy the passengers. They let us stay back here because they don't think anyone comes over here anyway. The Devil controls their minds, that's why they do things like that. They can't help it. The Devil uses them to prevent us from bringing peace and tranquility to the world. He has also given us some competition."

"How can there be competition at bringing peace to the world? Surely that's one thing everyone could cooperate on."

"Of course, my son, of course. But these are not missionaries of goodwill, like ourselves. These are crass merchants. Their only motive is greed. And they have the blessing of the officials."

"No!"

"I'm afraid it's true. Not only have we been pushed into the most remote section of each station, but the passengers must all pass by these merchants before they reach us. If they waste their money with the competition, we will sell no irises."

"What do they sell?"

"Rag dolls, my son. Ugly, shapeless and expensive. The Devil has entered the mind of every child in Europe and made them crave these nasty toys. Rag dolls are the enemy, make no mistake about it. If there are a lot of rag-doll salesmen, you're not going to be able to bring much tranquility to humanity. No one will want your irises."

"Let's see if I've got this. You keep track of how much peace I have brought to the world by how many irises I give away."

"That's right."

"But the more rag dolls there are in the station, the fewer irises I'll be able to move."

"That's right."

"Gosh, sir, I wish there was a way we could attract people over to us. Surely we can overcome the rag dolls!"

Mr. Ohm smiled knowingly.

"That's what this is for," he said, moving to a large wooden crate on the floor. Quickly he opened it. Out stepped a huge bird, a North American turkey. It looked around in confusion, shaking its wings, gobbling and making indignant noises in its throat. The turkey is not native to Europe, and the boy had never seen a bird like this before. He stepped back. George tied a cord around one of its legs and tethered it to the crate.

"What is it?" The boy's eyes were wide.

"That," Mr. Ohm said, "Is an eagle!"

"It's so big!"

"From America," Mr. Ohm continued. "Everything grows big over there. People here in Europe have never seen an American eagle. You'll have a crowd in no time."

"Aren't they dangerous?"

"Perfectly tame, my son. I'm told that my birds are the direct descendants of a flock kept by Ben Franklin himself. People will walk right past those rag doll salesmen to see an American eagle!"

"Are you sure it will work?"

"Absolutely. I used Paris as a test market. A certain number of people will come over to see one eagle. Twice as many will come to see two eagles. I can tell you exactly how many irises you'll distribute if I know how many eagles you have, and how many rag doll salesmen there are. When I go into a new market, I check how many rag doll salesmen there are, decide on a reasonable iris quota, and that's how I decide on the number of eagles to bring in.

"Or, say I want to keep track of the competition. I check the number of eagles and the iris sales and I can tell you in a minute how many rag-doll salesman are in the station. I have even made up a formula. I have it here somewhere... Oh well, I'll find it later. Now, I'll show you how to do it once more and then you're on your own. Just do whatever I do."

At that moment a group of Norwegian tourists entered the station. George turned and tried to cover his face with his hand, but one of them had already spotted him.

"Lars! Lars Thorvillson! Look everyone, it's Lars Thorvillson!" The whole group surrounded the two men in white robes.

"Ohm! My name is George Ohm! I've never even been to Norway!" The tourists laughed good naturedly.

"Why in the world are you dressed like that, Lars? Look, Cecilia, it's Lars Thorvillson from Stavanger!"

"Ohm! My name is George Ohm! Ohm, Ohm, Ohm!"

But they wouldn't give up. Finally he managed to escape the crowd, and raced out of the building, leaving the younger man to fend for himself. The tourists drifted away to check the stagecoach schedule.

The young man wasn't sure he understood what had just happened. He only wanted to bring peace to the world. The last words he heard from the master were "do whatever I do." For the rest of his life, he stood in that stage coach station giving away flowers and quietly saying, "Ohm, Ohm, Ohm."

Resistance In Series Circuits

Your flashlight is still too bright. You added a 100-ohm resistor, and it helped, but you and I are perfectionists and we're just not satisfied. We want to dim that flashlight some more.

Could we replace the 100-ohm resistor with a 200-ohm resistor?

Well, we could if we had a 200-ohm resistor. As it turns out, we got a good deal by buying a whole sack full of 100-ohm resistors and that's all we have. Being highly trained electronics experts, we figure we can make them work.

First we dig out the schematic of the flashlight:

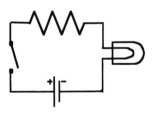

Say the light bulb has 500 ohms of resistance. The 100-ohm resistor and the 500-ohm bulb are in series (all the current has to go through them both to get through the circuit). We add the two together and realize there is a total of 600 ohms of resistance in our circuit.

You may be curious about how much current is flowing. Ohm's Law for current is:

$$I=E/R.$$

In our flashlight that translates into:

I (current) = 9 volts divided by 600 ohms

We divide nine by 600 and come up with .015 amps of current. It never occurred to Mr. Ohm that he'd wind up with less than one amp a lot of the time by choosing his units so casually. As a result of this poor planning, we've had to come up with the term "milliamp" which means "one-thousandth of an amp." Our flashlight circuit has 15 milli-amps of current, and that's too much for us. If we add another 100-ohm resistor in series with the first one like this:

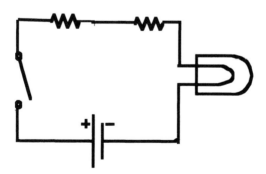

our flashlight will be dimmer. Using Ohm's Law we can see that now there is less than 13 milliamps of current. Each time we add a resistor in series, we reduce the current and the flashlight will become dimmer. If we wanted to add 1,000 ohms to a circuit we could string ten 100-ohm resistors end to end like Christmas tree lights.

But if we put the resistors side by side, like this:

99

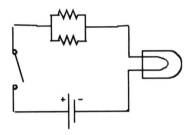

they're not in series any more. They're in parallel. Some electricity will go through one and some through the other. That second resistor is like the second footbridge over a canyon; it's not easy for buffaloes to get over, but it's easier than trying to make it on one footbridge. Obviously, adding resistors in parallel will not reduce our current. The more resistors we put into our flashlight in parallel, the brighter it's going to shine. You can't just add up the values of the resistors and see how much total resistance there is when they are arranged like that.

If you're not sure if resistors are in series or parallel, remember this: In a series circuit, every Greenie goes through every component in the same order. Trace the path of current on a schematic and your pencil will go through every component without backtracking and without lifting off the page. There are no choices to make, no forks in the road. In a parallel circuit there is at least one alternate route. Greenies can travel a complete circuit without going through every component.

To determine the total amount of resistance of resistors in series, just add them up.

Resistance in Parallel Circuits

You have one resistor. You add a second one in parallel. Your mind tells you that you've increased the total resistance in the circuit, but your mind is wrong. You have added an extra pathway for the current and done nothing to make the first pathway more difficult. If

100

none of the Greenies take the new second path, the resistance of the circuit will be no different than before. If even one or two of them can get through the new pathway, that's an improvement in the traffic flow. You have to think of parallel resistors as alternate routes that happen to have resistance, rather than additional obstacles in an established route. If all your resistors are the same size, the more of them you put into a circuit parallel to each other, the less total resistance you'll see in your circuit.

If the resistors are all the same size, this:

Has more resistance than this:

So how do you figure the total resistance of resistors in parallel? Someone who must have been a lot smarter than me figured it out, reduced it to a formula and wrote it down for the rest of us. I'm sure he was Norwegian. You don't need to remember it or even understand it to learn about electronics. There are, however, some very strange folks out there, people who would rather work out math problems than eat ice cream. To cover the unlikely possibility that one of them will read this book, I will include a formula from time to time. Believe me, we're all a lot safer if we keep those math-oriented guys pacified.

The formula for figuring total resistance in parallel circuits looks like this:

$$R \text{ (total)} = \frac{1}{1/R1 + 1/R2 + 1/R3 \text{ ...(etc.)}}$$

Let's assume we have three resistors in parallel, and each one is three ohms:

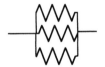

To figure their overall resistance, we put the number three, (for three ohms) in place of R1, R2, and R3:

$$R = \frac{1}{1/3 + 1/3 + 1/3}$$

The addition part is easy:

$$R = \frac{1}{1} = 1$$

Total resistance is one ohm. As you can imagine, I had to experiment a little to find an example that worked out that neatly. Let's do another one:

50 Ohms

25 Ohms

$$R = \frac{1}{1/R1 + 1/R2} = \frac{1}{1/50 + 1/25} = \frac{1}{3/50} = 16.66 \text{ Ohms}$$

Okay, so I did that one with a calculator, just like you did. Now you have the formula; my book has been legitimized by the inclusion of fancy-looking mathematics; some of you less adventurous readers have been left whimpering by the roadside; and, all the math junkies have been given their fix. Don't memorize the formula. You can always look it up. The important thing to remember is that the total resistance of resistors in parallel will always be less than the smallest resistor.

What?

I said, the total resistance of resistors in parallel will always be less than the smallest resistor.

Think about it.

Belinda

"Oh no!" I thought. I didn't need to open my eyes. I could feel cold stone beneath me, my neck was stiff and the air smelled old and damp. There were no bird sounds, no lake sounds. I knew what I was going to see.

"Welcome back," the thin voice said in its peculiar whispering way. I shivered.

"Good to be back," I said, sitting up and rubbing my neck. It was the same dungeon, with the same torch light flickering on the walls, the same simple table with two chairs. The Magician stood as before and motioned toward the table. I got up stiffly and obeyed his unspoken command.

"I would like you to meet someone," the Magician rasped as I sat at the table. He turned and stepped back. "This is Belinda."

Standing shyly behind the old man was a young woman of extraordinary beauty. Her gown was dark against her pale skin, her hair was long and black. Her face was perfect; smooth and innocent as a child's with eyes that seemed inhumanly large and soft. Bambi eyes, I thought.

Yet Belinda was obviously no child. She walked toward me and her body moved with wonderfully orchestrated sensuality beneath the simple gown. When she was near enough that I could smell her gentle perfume, she smiled. I swear, my heart stopped flat, my mouth went dry and I would have been happy to die, right then and there.

"Belinda is my assistant," the Magician said, and I thought I detected a faint hint of amusement in his voice. I pulled myself together.

103

"Pleased to meet you," I said, shaking her absolutely perfect hand.

"Me too," she said softly.

"Belinda will provide the things we need to make our work more comfortable," the Magician said. "I believe we could use some coffee as we begin, don't you?"

I nodded as Belinda turned and walked gracefully away, disappearing into a shadowy opening in the dismal rock wall. I could not take my eyes from the spot.

"She'll be back soon enough with coffee," the old man said. "Do I detect a certain amount of voltage in you?"

"She seems like a very intelligent person," I said.

"Don't mistake me," the Magician said. "You are still completely expendable to me. But you have made an effort to provide me with the information I need. Therefore it is reasonable that you be rewarded with certain creature comforts."

"You mean…"

"I mean the coffee."

"Oh."

Belinda returned with hot coffee, perfect coffee, as far as I was concerned. Then she moved away again and sat in the shadows.

"Shall we begin?" The man's questions always seemed to lack the element of choice in their answers. I took a deep breath and turned my mind back to electronics.

"Okay, we already talked about voltage, current, resistance, magnetism, inductance and capacitance, right?"

"Yes."

"Well, that's pretty much all the characteristics of electricity. From there we go on to building circuits that use those characteristics."

"Whenever you're ready," he said, a bit impatiently.

"There are two kinds of circuits," I went on. "Series and parallel. When things are in series that means that they are placed end to end." Current goes through each component in order, and all the current goes through each component."

"Component?"

"Right. A component is any little electrical device, any part of a circuit. We put components together into circuits."

"I understand. When you string components together, one after another you have made a series circuit. Then what's a parallel circuit?"

"A parallel circuit is when components are side by side, so that some electricity goes through one and some through the other. The current in each one will be moving sort of parallel to each other."

"Like railroad tracks?"

"Well, no, not exactly." I said. He wasn't getting it.

"Aren't railroad tracks parallel?"

"Well, sure they are. Okay, look. The wooden railroad ties are also parallel, aren't they? Picture each railroad tie as an electrical component. Maybe one's a resistor, the next one's a light bulb, the next one is a speaker and then another resistor and so on. Now we hook one rail to one side of our battery and the other rail to the other side. Our Greenies go down one rail and some of them will go through each component on their way to the other rail. Those components are hooked up 'in parallel.'"

"Greenies?"

"I mean electrons. Forget that I said Greenies."

"Hmm," he said.

Quickly I went on. "There are only a few ways to make electricity. The most common way is to move a magnet near a wire. All electrical generators and alternators use this principle.

"We also use chemicals to make electricity. Just about any two different metals will create electricity if you put them in an acid, for example.

"The other ways of producing electricity are less important. Friction can create static electricity. Sunlight creates electricity when it shines on certain materials. Two different metals pressed together and heated can create electricity. And some crystals make a tiny current under pressure."

"Why do those things create electricity?" the Magician asked.

"Does it matter?"

The Magician thought about that for a moment and I noticed the torch flickering, getting much brighter, flaring dangerously high.

"I guess not," he said, and the torch settled down again.

"The truth is, I don't exactly understand why those things make electricity myself, and I don't think anyone else does either. On the other hand, I don't understand the chemistry behind the sensation of hunger, either, but I can recognize it and satisfy it as well as any bio-chemical engineer."

"A good point," he said, and motioned to the shadows. Immediately Belinda brought us each a jelly roll and more coffee. She also smiled at me again, an absolutely perfect smile, shy and yet friendly, and revealed a wonderful set of lovely, delicate teeth. She was obviously under-employed, I thought. Then it occurred to me that she might not be an employee at all. She might be a captive. Or an illusion of some sort. I rubbed the spot on my forehead where my eyebrows used to be and watched her return to the shadows. The Magician, with all his apparent powers, did not need someone to carry jelly rolls for him. She was there for my benefit, somehow. If she was an illusion, I thought, the Magician is very good at his job. He tapped his fingers on the table top.

"There are three main ways we convert electricity into work," I said with a sigh, and bit into the jelly roll. I could still detect Belinda's perfume clinging faintly to it, but forced myself to concentrate. "When electricity goes through anything, resistance causes it to heat up. This is used in all kinds of devices to produce heat. The part that gets hot is called the heating element, or, if it's real small, the filament. Heating elements can get so hot they glow. Light bulbs use glowing filaments to produce light.

"The second way to make electricity work for you is to create electromagnets. Electromagnets turning on and off make electric motors rotate, music speakers vibrate, aquarium bubblers pump air and electric razors cut your whiskers. If an electrical device creates motion, it probably is using an electromagnet.

"Some materials glow in the presence of electricity. Fluorescent lights and television screens use this to produce light."

"Television?"

"Right. Television is like... well, everybody has a television." I didn't want to try to explain the electronics or the social phenomenon of television. "It's like a big message board. Everyone in the country gets information from television. A television screen lights up because it's coated with a substance that glows when electricity hits it."

"Oh."

"The other ways to use electricity are minor. Some crystals expand slightly when you run a current through them. A bimetallic strip will get colder in response to electricity. The molecules of a liquid crystal will align themselves one way or another depending on the charge; you can take weird photographs using static electricity instead of light; and a whole subculture thinks that plants grow better if there's an electrical current near them. I doubt if any of those are used in your time machine."

"No, they're not," the Magician said with a faraway look in his eyes. "But I can tell you this: I have seen the future. One of the effects that you consider minor today will become vastly important in the future. A whole industry will arise from it, and a few individuals will become fabulously wealthy as a result of it."

"Someone who has read my book, perhaps?"

"Perhaps," he said softly. "Perhaps. Continue."

"Okay. Now we get to the drawings. Each component has a symbol. A conductor is a line, for example, a resistor is a jagged line, like shark teeth. We put these symbols together to draw a plan of an electrical circuit and call it a schematic diagram."

"This doesn't seem so difficult," he said.

"It's not, really," I said, finishing my jelly roll. "Now we get to Ohm's Law. If you increase the resistance in a circuit, less current will go through. On the other hand, if you increase the voltage, more current will go through. If you know two of the three characteristics, (voltage, resistance and current) you can figure what the third must be using Ohm's Law. Voltage equals current times resistance; Current equals voltage divided by resistance; Resistance equals voltage divided by current. The abbreviation is 'E=IR'. That's Ohm's Law."

"I hate mathematics!" the Magician said, through tightly clenched teeth. I was sure I felt my chair slowly lifting off the floor, and the torch was dancing crazily.

"I do too!" I said emphatically. "Believe me, if I didn't think it would help you with your project, I wouldn't even mention it. Here, take my calculator. I'll write down the formulas you might need. With the calculator it'll be a snap." I felt my chair lowering again.

"I've heard about these calculators..." he said with some interest. "They're great!" I said. "They make it fun." I showed him how to use the calculator. He caught on very quickly. A bit sadly, I realized I would never get that calculator back.

"Look," I said. "There's only two more things I've written about, but they involve a little math." I wanted to warn him so he wouldn't get upset. He made me nervous when he got upset.

"Can I use my calculator on them?" I noticed that he already called it "his" calculator. I sighed and decided it was a small price to pay.

"You bet," I said. "When resistors are in series with each other, to figure their total resistance, just add them up."

"Let's try some examples!" He seemed eager. I gave him several examples, he did them quickly on the calculator. "That's fun!" he said. "How do you add up resistors when they're in parallel?"

"Here's the formula," I said and wrote:

$$R = \frac{1}{1/R1 + 1/R2 + 1/R3 \ldots \text{etc.}}$$

Surprisingly, it didn't seem to bother him. He quickly did some examples on the calculator and seemed rather pleased with himself. Then he sat back.

"You have done well," he said. "If you continue to be well prepared at our next meetings, you may survive. It is interesting that the more resistors you add in parallel, the less the total resistance. It smacks of a paradox, and, of course, I love paradoxes.

"I will leave you now. But, as I believe in punishment, so I also understand the value of rewards. You have earned a reward." He turned to the shadows. "Belinda!" he commanded. The lovely young lady approached us. My mind reeled and my cheeks felt hot. What sort of reward did the Magician have in mind? I turned to ask, but he had simply vanished. Belinda came closer, each movement a poem, each graceful step a symphony. I was bewitched by this woman, this vision, this amazing dream that moved like a warm liquid and glowed like some luscious tropical flower. Now I would discover who she was, why she was there. The Magician had said "reward." What had he meant?

She stood very close to me now. My heart was pounding. She reached her hand out to me.

"Eggs," she whispered.

"What?" I responded in confusion. She smiled sweetly.

"Eggs," she repeated, touching my shoulder with her small, lovely hand.

"I don't understand..."

Suddenly she was shaking my shoulder, the dungeon was becoming lost in the darkness, and her voice was becoming distorted.

"Oh no!" I thought, as I realized what was happening. I shook my head and tried to fight it, but it was no use. As I opened my eyes, Mike was shaking my shoulder.

"I said, your eggs are ready, bro'. Rise and shine!"

"Oh no!" I said out loud.

"I think you were having a nightmare, man. You were sure squirming around. No need to thank me," my green friend said, holding up his hand as if to stop me. "Back safe in reality. Have some breakfast."

Eggs never looked worse to me in my life.

A Parking Lot on Lover's Leap

The capacitor is the cheese sandwich of electrical components. Each slice of bread is a conductor, and the cheese is a very thin insulator. The slices of bread (the conductors) are called "plates" and the cheese that separates them is called the "dielectric." "Dielectric" is one of the most charming bits of jargon, because it sounds so darned official, yet means nothing more than "an insulator that separates the two plates in a capacitor." Air can be the dielectric, paper can be the dielectric. Glass, plastic, mica, wood, polyester or even a vacuum can be the dielectric. Actually, you could probably use cheese. Of course, some things work better than others.

If you separate two pieces of aluminum foil with a piece of wax paper, you have built a working capacitor.

But what good is it?

When you attach the aluminum foil plates to opposite sides of a battery, you have an open circuit. The wax paper dielectric is a good insulator: Current can't flow through it. But it is so thin, the Greenies can still hear that party music, they can feel the voltage. If they feel the voltage, they'll travel as far as they can. They'll drive from the negative terminal to the aluminum foil and spread out, looking for a way to get through, until the foil can't hold any more of the little fellows. At the same time, whatever Greenies were already on the other aluminum foil plate will abandon their parking spots and boogie on down to the positive side of the battery, where the party is.

My term for those Greenies that started out on the positive plate is "lucky Greenies."

At any rate, in that first instant, a capacitor has no effect on the rest of the circuit. Greenies are moving toward it, Greenies are moving away from it. It might as well be a wire.

But it sneaks up on you.

As Greenies fill up the plate, it gets tougher to find a spot. It's developing a negative charge, which tends to repel new revelers. Within a fraction of a second, everyone knows that the road is closed, traffic is backed up all the way to the negative terminal, and the dielectric has shown us its true face. It's an insulator, a party-pooper, a current stopper.

As the curtain falls on our little story, one plate has a negative charge, one plate has a positive charge, and the dielectric is laughing at us all. No current is flowing. The capacitor is said to be "charged."

At this point, if we provide some path between the two plates, the Greenies will take it, equalizing the charges. Greenies from the over-full parking lot on the first plate will drive to the vacant second plate and park there.

110

There is a certain logic to the symbol for a capacitor:

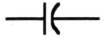

Suppose we put a capacitor and a resistor in parallel in a circuit: We close the switch. Greenies rush to the capacitor plate that is nearest the negative battery terminal. That appears to be an easy path. Others choose to go through the resistor. Within a fraction of a second, the capacitor will be fully charged. There will be no room for new Greenies. When that happens, all the electricity will skip the capacitor route altogether and will travel through the resistor. The capacitor has acted like a resistor whose resistance increases over time. If the plates are large enough, and the parallel resistor small enough, it could take several minutes for the capacitor to become fully charged. As it does, more and more current will flow through the resistor, while less and less flows through the section of the circuit that includes the capacitor.

In an interesting side note, some large capacitors can store huge numbers of Greenies. In fact, if you happen to grab both ends of one of them, they will fry you dead. Do not play footsies with big capacitors. Some of them can "hold a charge" for over a month.

Any insulator can be defeated by a very large need-to-party, and our dielectric is no exception. At some voltage, any dielectric will break down – spring a leak as it were, and let those Greenies through. Usually this is permanent damage, and you have to replace the capacitor. It is wise to know the "break-down voltage" of the capacitors you use so you can prevent the problem. Of course, sometimes it just happens.

Perhaps the neatest capacitor in the world (aside from clouds) takes advantage of its own break-down voltage. Neon bulbs are little capacitors that use neon gas as the dielectric to separate two little metal plates. When the break-down voltage is reached, electricity streams from plate to plate. Neon gas glows red when electricity travels through it. Little neon bulbs are handy. The distance between the plates determines the break-down voltage. As long as you're below that

111

voltage, no light. Once you reach it, bingo! Your little light goes on. Since you don't damage the gas, it will work over and over again, telling you when you reach a certain voltage. Science teachers don't think of neon bulbs as capacitors. They focus their attention on the ionizing of the neon gas. Find one and argue with him.

Capacitors are rated in terms of how large a charge they can hold. Both the amount of voltage between the plates and how much current would flow if you discharged it through a conductor have to be considered. The capacity is really how much energy can be stored in a capacitor. Capacitance is measured in "farads," after the Norwegian scientist "Jon Johnson." When he realized that no one was going to listen to a scientist whose first name was pronounced "Yawn," Mr. Johnson adopted the name of Michael Faraday, and farad comes from that. This is an interesting historical footnote that you will not find in most electronics books.

Once again, someone arbitrarily picked a size for the unit and it turned out to be too big for common usage. Therefore we hear a lot about micro-farads (one millionth of a farad), and even pico-farads (one trillionth of a farad).

I mean, it was *way* too big.

Fun Times in Fjordland

The Olafsons like to play a little game when families visit them from the city; They think of it as a practical joke. If a visiting family brags about their athletic children, the Olafsons propose a race: one mile, our best kid against your best kid. The Olafson kids do not look athletic. The visitors always fall for it.

After placing the usual bets (50 pound of lutefisk is standard) the two families go down to the high school racetrack. The track is just like any you'd find around the football field at a typical American high school. It is exactly a quarter of a mile, a mile race is four laps. The only little oddity is that this track has a chain-link fence right across it that's nearly 20 feet high. The fencing contractor who enclosed the school yard either mis-read the plans, or got carried away by the sheer joy of putting up chain-link – no one's sure. The school can't tear it down, either, because it's considered material evidence in their lawsuit against the contractor. So, for now, the local high school track has a dead end. You can run one lap just fine; the fence only blocks the track in one place before it wanders out and stops in the middle of the football field. No one expects this year's track team to break any records in the mile.

The rules to the bet are simple. No fair going around the fence; Your guy goes first, we'll all time him; Whoever gets the best time wins. Put your lutefisk where your mouth is.

The visitors look up at the chain link fence. Twenty feet is a tall fence. Even if they start with their back pressed against the fence, they'll have to climb it three times to run a mile. On the other hand, the fence is just as much an obstacle for the Olafson boy as it is for them. And, of course, there's 50 pounds of lutefisk at stake.

They agree to the terms. Their boy starts running. He's making good time, in fact, he runs like a racehorse. Unfortunately, he climbs fences about as well as a racehorse, too. It takes him 10 minutes to get halfway up that fence.

But he's a plucky lad; although his body aches, he keeps trying. It turns out that the fence is just tall enough to trigger his fear of heights, and terror becomes a factor. Nevertheless, he endures the torture and he does his best. After another five minutes or so of agony, everyone agrees that the fence has won, and the young athlete carefully works his way back down, exhausted and more than a little embarrassed.

But the visitors aren't ready to just hand over 50 pounds of lutefisk. No sir. The Olafson boy hasn't run any mile either, and they're not going to admit defeat until he does.

So Ollie, the Olafson boy, starts trotting around the field. He's careful to start with his back pressed up against the fence. There are smug smiles exchanged among members of the visiting family. These smiles vanish when Ollie finishes his first lap, touches the fence, then turns around and runs his second lap in the opposite direction.

The air is filled with Norwegian curses, the simple and polite translation of which is that the visitors think this is less than fair. The Olafsons are, as always, shocked by this response. Certainly no one ever said that you had to run the entire mile clockwise. Goodness, couldn't they see there was a chain-link fence across the track? Why, it would slow you down terribly if you had to climb that thing every lap. No, the rules were that you had to run a mile, on the track, without going around the fence. That obviously meant that when you reach the fence, you turn around and run your next lap the opposite direction.

"Trickery!" The visitors scream, while young Ollie plods around his final lap. It's not an especially good time for a mile, a little over nine minutes. Still, it's one of Ollie's better times, and once again, it was good enough to win 50 pounds of lutefisk.

The Olafsons seldom have repeat visitors.

The moral of this little story is simple:

"It's not always how fast you run; sometimes it's how well you understand your bets."

The Capacity to be Green

"What's lutefisk?" Mike asked, after reading the chapter.

"Lutefisk is a traditional Scandinavian food. It's really codfish, preserved with salt and dried. To prepare it, you soak it in lye, and boil it all day until it's the consistency of a jellyfish. Then you force your children to eat it at Christmas so they learn about their heritage, while the grownups have turkey or ham. Great stuff."

"Hmm," Mike said thoughtfully. Finally he spoke again. "Do you suppose anyone might have read that last chapter without understanding that it was really about capacitors?"

"Nah," I said. "How could they misunderstand? It seemed pretty obvious to me."

"Well, to me too, of course," Mike said. "But then, you didn't actually use the word 'capacitor.' Don't you think maybe some of the younger kids might miss the whole thing?"

"I suppose it's possible," I sighed. "But then why would I put a story about Norwegians racing around a track with a chain-link fence across it in a book about electronics if it wasn't about capacitors?"

"Why don't you just tell them. You know, just in case."

"Oh, all right," I said. "The fence is the dielectric of course. It's very difficult for a runner to get past a fence, and it's very difficult for electricity to get past a dielectric. So, current flows until it gets to it. Then it stops. Unless, of course, you reverse the direction of the current. Then it will move in the opposite direction until it's stopped again by the dielectric."

"I think you can put it even more simply."

I took a deep breath.

"Direct current gets stopped cold by a capacitor. But alternating current can work around it."

"That's better. Now tell them how the frequency of AC affects it and we'll go fishing."

"Okay. Alternating current is like a runner who has to turn around every time he hears a whistle. If the whistle blows often enough, he'll never get to the chain-link fence. If the whole track is full of runners like that, and you blow the whistle every three seconds, the fence will have very little effect on any of them. A lot of dust will be raised and any weeds on the track will be trampled. On the other hand, if you only blow the whistle every half hour, or if you never blow it, the fence will stop everyone.

"The slower the frequency, the more effect a capacitor will have. If the capacitor is large enough and the frequency is fast enough, the capacitor will have no effect at all on alternating current.

"A capacitor acts like a resistor that has very little resistance the first instant current enters it, but increases in resistance with time. When you reverse the direction of the current, you start over with little resistance. Direct current will get stopped cold, after that first instant. Alternating current will not. The higher the frequency, the less of an obstacle a capacitor becomes."

"Just like in the Norwegian race track," Mike said.

"Just like that. Let's fish."

Determining Capacitance

There are three things that affect how much capacitance a capacitor will have:

1. How much surface area do the plates have?
2. How close together are they?
3. What is the dielectric?

The more surface area the plates have, the more room there is for Greenies, and the more charge they can store. More surface equals more parking spots equals more capacitance.

The closer the two plates are to each other the easier it is to hear the music, or feel the voltage across the dielectric barrier. Therefore, the closer together the plates, the more capacitance. Of course, the closer they are, the lower the break-down voltage, too.

And some materials work better as the dielectric than others. The material must be a good insulator, yet it must also let Greenies hear the party, feel the voltage. A cardboard wall lets sound through, for example, but it won't keep out dedicated party crashers. A brick wall would keep you safe, but nobody would hear your music through it, either. On the other hand, a chain-link fence, with barbed wire on top, will deter party crashers pretty effectively while still allowing you to keep the whole neighborhood awake. Wax paper is a good dielectric, air isn't bad, polyester works, and so does mica. Lots of things work. The better it works, the greater its "dielectric constant." Air has a dielectric constant of "one," and everything else is compared to that.

As you combine capacitors in circuits, remember what makes them have more or less capacitance and it will be easy to see how combinations of more than one will behave.

If you add a capacitor in parallel to another, you effectively increase the surface area. You know that more surface area means more capacitance.

To determine total capacitance of several parallel capacitors, simply add up their individual values.

When you put capacitors in series, however, you are effectively increasing the distance between the plates. Greenies have to sense the voltage across more than one dielectric. They have to hear the music through more than one wall. Since increasing the distance between plates decreases the amount of capacitance, putting capacitors in series actually decreases the total capacitance.

The formula for figuring out the total capacitance of capacitors in series will look vaguely familiar to you:

$$C \text{ (total)} = \frac{1}{1/C1 + 1/C2 + 1/C3...(\text{etc.})}$$

It's the same program we used to determine resistance in parallel circuits. Only the names have been changed. The math is the same. Remember that we use it for resistors in parallel and capacitors in series. If you can do one you can do the other, without learning anything new.

That is a happy coincidence that proves you and I have been leading pure lives.

Dan says, "I'd Rather Not be in Your Book"

I am writing this the first week of October, 1986. I mention the date only so you can check out my story. The nights have become too cold for camping, but the book isn't done. Mike hasn't been able to return home yet, and I haven't seen either the Magician or Belinda for a while. Mike and I decided that we ought to rent a cabin in the area so we don't freeze to death and just keep plugging away. What we'd like to do is move our little operation to a college campus somewhere, so we could eat a cheeseburger at the student union when we felt like it, or shoot some pool. That would also give us a college library as a resource. Reluctantly, we both agreed that Mike's green skin would attract too much attention at any campus (with the possible exceptions of the University of Colorado and Berkeley, where strange things are fairly commonplace). Brigham Young was out of the question. So we rented a cabin.

After we did, I drove into town to get supplies: beer, Cheetos, marshmallows – the staples. I also picked up a newspaper. One little

117

article made me break out in a cold sweat and prevented me from sleeping all night long. I was terrified. You may have missed it, but it was there. I still have the clipping.

The most popular TV newsman in the country was stopped by two men in business suits as he walked down a New York street. "Kenneth, what's the frequency?" they asked him. "What's the frequency, Kenneth?"

He assured them that he was not Kenneth. They asked again, and when he could not answer, they started to beat him up. Luckily, he escaped. All over the country people must have looked up from their dinner, shook their heads at the six o'clock news and said, "Hmm, how odd," and then promptly forgot the incident.

Not me. My name is Kenneth, although everyone calls me Kenn. I'm writing a book about electronics, which includes a lot of talk about frequencies. And one person might have a question for me about it, a person who wouldn't hesitate to beat me up, or anyone else. A person who could probably create two thugs out of dried lizard skin and toad tongues. But why hadn't the Magician just come directly to me?

Then I realized that I had moved. Our old campsite was vacant. Maybe he couldn't find me!

At first I felt a certain relief at that thought. I was safe. Then I thought again. The old fellow was smart enough to get a very specific message, with my name, on all the television networks and newspapers in the country for free. Microsoft can't do that. He had a question for me, and he wanted an answer. Maybe he wasn't especially efficient in the unfamiliar world of the 20th century, but I decided it would be foolish to underestimate him. Sooner or later, he'd find me. And, if he thought I was hiding from him, he'd be irritated.

I stayed awake all night long in our new cabin, staring into the fireplace. I kept the fire blazing, and my hair smelled like pine-wood smoke for days.

The next day I went back to our old campsite, and nailed a note to a tree explaining our move. With mixed feelings I drew a map showing our cabin's location.

Then I returned and wrote like crazy.

The Coil

If you want a lot of self-inductance, coil up your wire. The lines of magnetic force that grow and shrink around the wire will have no choice but to cut across the loops and cause little voltages that will always be contrary to your main intent. If you try to increase current, these little voltages will oppose you. If you try to decrease current, they will try to keep it going. A coil will oppose any change in current.

To increase a coil's self-inductance, add more loops of wire, squeeze the loops together tightly, or add an iron core.

When we want more self-inductance in a circuit, we add a coil of wire. A coil is considered a component, and its symbol is this:

I'm not sure how you'll remember the symbol, but perhaps you'll think of something.

So why would anybody want more self-inductance in a circuit? Well, maybe you want to protect your other components from a violent surge of current. No problem. Add a coil. Surges of current are the things that coils stop the best. The more dramatic the surge, the more self-inductance it will inspire, and therefore the more opposition it will encounter in the coil. It's like Chinese handcuffs: the harder you pull on them, the tighter they hold. The only way to escape is to relax.

Or, suppose it's important for the DC current in a circuit to be constant, not changing with every little distraction. A coil can help there, too. As your current overcomes the initial self-inductance of the coil, it stores energy in the form of the magnetic field that now surrounds it. If there is a minor, temporary reduction in current, some of this energy will be returned to the circuit by the shrinking field, keeping it going. On the other hand, a little surge in current will have to overcome the self-inductance of the coil, and will also be to some extent nullified. At least its energy will be stored and released into the circuit more gradually.

Coils tend to stabilize the current in a circuit. They tend to oppose any change in the status quo. They don't like it when current varies.

"Aha!" I hear you exclaiming. "Then what do coils think of alternating current?"

The simple answer is: "Not much." Alternating current is constantly changing. It builds to a peak, tapers off, changes direction, builds to a peak and tapers off again. A coil opposes all of those plans making it difficult for alternating current to get through one. If a coil has enough self-inductance, and the current is reversing itself quickly, AC won't be able to get past a coil at all. It will act like an open switch, an electrical dead end.

A coil acts like a big resistor the first instant current hits it, but its resistance decreases quickly. This is the exact opposite of a capacitor, which develops more and more resistance as it becomes charged.

When the frequency of AC current is slow, some current gets through a coil. If it takes one second to overcome the self-inductance, and the current reverses once every five seconds, for a few seconds each cycle the coil will have little effect. If the current is reversing itself a thousand times a second, however, it's never headed one direction long enough to do anything. self-inductance in the coil will always be maximum. You'll be lucky if a few bedraggled Greenies stumble out either end of that coil, and those that do will be frazzled, irritable, and probably not good company.

The frequency of the AC will determine how much effect a coil will have in a circuit.

This brings up the most interesting use for coils, and another wonderful bit of jargon. You can use a coil to block AC from getting from one part of a circuit to another. You can, in fact, eliminate alternating current altogether from your circuit. Kill it, smother it, destroy it.

Choke it, if you will.

Coils that are used to eliminate AC above a certain frequency are called "chokes."

Capacitors and Coils Disguised as Resistors

The frequency of the AC will determine how much effect a coil or capacitor will have. These two components are not passive like a resistor. They react to the frequency, they react to each other. The same coil or capacitor will behave differently in different circuits.

Therefore, we can't just call their opposition to current flow "resistance," although that's what it acts like. No sir. This is an opportunity for jargon. Because they "react" to frequency, the opposition provided by capacitors and coils is called "reactance."

Capacitors have "capacitive reactance." It acts just like resistance, except that it is smallest the first instant current flows. The higher the frequency, the less the capacitive reactance.

Coils have "inductive reactance." It also acts just like resistance, except that it's greatest the first instant current flows. The higher the frequency the greater the inductive reactance.

Resistors have plain old resistance. Resistance does not change no matter what the frequency.

Reactance is measured in ohms. You have to know the frequency of AC in a circuit, as well as the capacitance or inductance of the component to figure how much reactance it will have.

Because capacitive reactance is greatest when inductive reactance is smallest, and vice versa, when you put both into a circuit, they tend to offset each other. Figuring the total amount of opposition becomes more fun.

The solution is obvious: more jargon!

The total opposition to current in an AC circuit is called "impedance." You can think of impedance as AC resistance; it is measured in ohms. The only difference is that impedance takes the frequency into account. Impedance is resistance, plus the effect of capacitive reactance, plus the effect of inductive reactance.

You will get the best sound out of your stereo if you make sure that the impedance of the amplifier is the same as the impedance of the speakers. This is called "matching" the impedances. Some of the terrible sounding systems you have heard might have been made up of fabulous components that simply did not have the same impedance.

Don't Waterski Inside a Coil

A motorboat is cruising across a lake. At the helm we see a familiar face: It is none other than Bruce the Duck. He is wearing a little captain's hat and the wind ruffles his feathers. There is pride in his eyes, and a smile on his beak. He is testing various routes for the big motorboat race coming up next week. The race committee has arranged buoys in the water to mark the course.

The race is a bit odd. When a light flashes on the console of your boat, you have to turn around and go the opposite direction. This is because they could not afford to rent a large lake, yet they wanted to have a long race. It did not occur to them to make the course circular. They are still trying to work out the details. The winner is the guy whose boat odometer shows that he's traveled the most distance during the race.

Two elements are involved, which is twice as many as the committee is comfortable with. The first is how to lay out the course. Should it be straight, or serpentine, or what? The second is, how often should they send the signal for the boats to turn around? Should they let them go a long way each direction, or a short way? Should they make them reverse direction every minute or so, or every 10 seconds or so?

Bruce is helping them evaluate those choices. For this run they have arranged the buoys in an extremely curvy path, almost a zigzag route. And, they have decided to make Bruce turn around very often, once every 10 seconds.

They begin the test. Bruce guides his boat quickly and skillfully through those tight turns. Then he reverses. Then reverses again.

The unexpected result of this winding route, coupled with fast reversals, is that Bruce is churning up the water, creating big, powerful waves that he must constantly fight. He makes little progress at moving through the water; worse, the boat can't take the pounding, the engine gets wet, water rushes on board, soaks his lunch, and sinks the boat.

For just a moment, Bruce flails around in the water, screaming for help, watching the boat disappear into the dark green water beneath him. Then he remembers that he's a duck, regains his composure, and paddles calmly to shore wearing the dignified expression of a cat who has done something silly and uncatlike.

The committee decided, wisely, that if the race route looped around, they would have to keep the frequency of their reversals pretty slow. They also decided that if they were going to reverse directions quickly, they would have to stick to a straight course.

All agreed on one thing. They wished they had a bigger lake.

Determining Inductance

Inductance is measured in "henrys," after the famous Norwegian scientist Joseph Henry. You can figure out how many henrys a coil of wire has if you know how many loops there are, how close together the loops are, what the diameter of the coil is and how much resistance your wire has to start with. Then, of course, you have to know the formula. Shoot, if you knew all that, you could build your own coil, with however many henrys you wanted.

On the other hand, you can always just go down to the electronics store and buy a coil that tells you how many henrys it has on its label. I'm going to bet you'd rather do that right now, and skip all those formulas.

Of course, you will probably encounter circuits with more than one coil in them and you'll be eager to discover how much total inductance the circuit has. No problem.

Coils (or "inductors," as they're sometimes called) in series act like one long coil. First you overcome one, then the next one. Simply add their values together to get the total inductance:

one henry + one henry +one henry = three henrys

Coils in parallel act like resistors in parallel. Because there are alternate routes for the current, there is less total inductance. The formula may also look familiar:

$$L \text{ (total Inductance)} = \frac{1}{1/L1 + 1/L2 + 1/L3... \text{ (etc)}}$$

I've thought about the abbreviations quite a bit, and I think I've figured it out. In a peculiar jargonistic twist, the fellow who discovered that self-induced current always opposes a change in the primary current was a famous Norwegian scientist named H.F.E. Lenz. Anybody who would call himself that obviously liked abbreviations. Since Henry got the privilege of having the unit of measurement named after him, I think that Lenz got the distinction of having the abbreviation named after him. Therefore, when you see a capital "L" in a formula, they're talking about inductance, and it's measured in henrys. One must admire their creativity. When you replace each "L" with a real number, it will be so many henrys, and the answer will be in henrys. That's "henry," abbreviated "L."

If you think about it, it makes some sense. They couldn't use "I" for "inductance," because "I" is the abbreviation for current, which is measured in amperes. Perhaps someone suggested changing the abbreviation for current to "C", to free the capital "I" for use with inductance. Couldn't do it. "C" is used for capacitance. So why didn't they use "F," short for "farad," for capacitance so they could use "C" for current, so they could use "I" for inductance?

Because they didn't think of it, that's why.

I don't find it confusing... do you? The units and abbreviations all make perfect sense:

"I" stands for current, measured in amps;
"C" stands for capacitance, measured in farads;
"R" stands for resistance, measured in ohms;
"E" stands for voltage, measure (oddly enough) in volts; and
"L" stands for inductance, measured in henrys.

And they will tell you, with a straight face, that electronics requires a logical mind.

The Cheeseburger and the Tiger

You are locked in a plain white room. You cannot escape. In front of you are two doors. One door is marked "AC," the other door is marked "DC." Between them, two electrical wires come out of the wall with bare copper exposed at their ends. You must determine whether those wires are hooked up to a source of direct current or alternating current, then open the correct door.

Your captors are cruel, having formerly been physical education teachers at a junior high school. For the last month they have put you on the famous Norwegian Diet (all the lutefisk you can eat, but nothing else). You have lost 25 pounds, and you weren't overweight to start with. Behind one of those doors is a three-quarter pound cheeseburger, juicy, fresh off the grill, loaded with pickles, onions, tomato... the works. You would kill for that cheeseburger.

Behind the other door is a tiger, who has been on the same diet. Not only has he lost a lot of weight, but the experience has ruined his disposition. This is not a mellow beast. Besides being ravenously hungry, he has developed an intense personal hatred of all things Norwegian. They have told him that your name is Lars, so you want to get this right the first time.

The cheeseburger is behind the door marked for the kind of current source those wires are hooked up to.

The only other item in the room is a cardboard box full of various electrical components. You have a copy of this book. You turn to this page, and this is what you see:

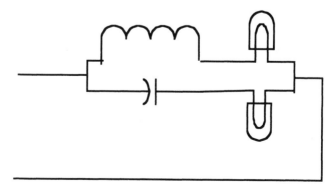

125

Your captors have told you what the voltage will be. They have also told you what frequency it will be, if it's AC. Since, by this time, you have finished the entire book, with this information you know what size components to use. You will build this little device, hook one end of it to one wire and the other end to the other wire. Then you will watch to see which light comes on and stays on.

That will tell you which door to pick.

If you're not sure how to interpret the results, I suggest you go back a couple of chapters and reread, before you risk your lunch on eenie-meenie-miny-mo.

The Transformer: More Than Meets the Eye

When two coils are placed close to each other for the specific purpose of letting the current in one induce a current in the other, we call the thing a "transformer." Not surprisingly, the symbol for a transformer is:

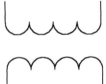

The two coils can be side by side, as you'd expect from the symbol. Or they can be placed end to end. You can even put a small coil inside a larger coil. As long as the magnetic field from the first coil (called the "primary coil") moves across the second coil ("the secondary") it will induce current in it by mutual inductance.

The primary is hooked up to a source of voltage. The secondary is not attached to any outside source of voltage. It receives its power only from the first coil, by inductance.

Because alternating current produces lines of force that are constantly moving, AC is the ideal stuff to use in transformers. If alternating current is going through the primary, you will find alternating current in the secondary, moving in time to the first current, even though they are not directly connected.

We can increase the efficiency of a transformer by providing some iron for the magnetism to move through. Iron has less "reluctance" than air. The symbol for an "iron core transformer" is the same, but with two parallel lines drawn between the coils.

This "magnetic coupling" is more efficient than you might guess. Even though the two wires are insulated from each other, if the current in the primary is strong enough to knock you down, the current in the secondary probably will be, too.

Transformers can be used to connect two circuits together when one might have some DC which you want to isolate from the other. Only the AC will induce current. Whatever DC might have been in the first circuit will be left behind, while the AC continues onward.

When the primary and secondary coils don't have the same number of loops (or "turns"), an odd thing happens. If the secondary has more turns, each line of flux will cross the secondary wire more times. That means it will induce more voltage than before. Every time a line of flux moves across a wire, it causes a little more voltage. On the other hand, the turns we just added increase the self-inductance in the secondary, which restricts the flow of current. So, if the secondary has more turns than the primary, you will discover more voltage in the secondary, but less current.

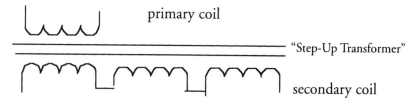

primary coil

"Step-Up Transformer"

secondary coil

Would you like for me to do that one more time?

It is hard for AC to go through a coil. The more turns in the coil, the harder it is. So, the more turns there are in our secondary, the less current will be able to get through it. We have increased the inductive reactance of our secondary, given it more impedance, more resistance, if you will.

Still, every time a line of flux moves across a wire, it induces a voltage, creates a desire to move among the Greenies, whether it's easy for them to move or not. So, the more turns there are in the secondary, the more voltage will be induced.

A transformer with more turns in the secondary than in the primary is called a "step-up" transformer. It steps-up, or increases, the voltage. It pays the price for this in reduced current.

There is an exact relationship between the relative number of turns in the two coils, and the change in voltage. If the secondary has 10 times as many turns as the primary, it will have 10 times as much voltage. On the other hand, it will only have one-tenth the current.

A step-down transformer is just the opposite. The secondary has fewer turns than the primary. Now it's easy for AC to go through, but there are fewer loops for the magnetism to cross. A step-down transformer will have less voltage in its secondary than in its primary, but more current.

primary coil

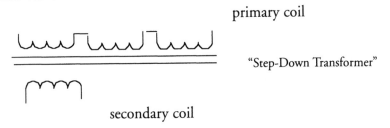

"Step-Down Transformer"

secondary coil

The transformer is obviously a pretty neat thing. By using it we can change (or transform) one voltage into another. The fact that AC can be manipulated so easily with transformers is one advantage it has over DC in many applications. High voltages lose less power over long distances. So, when we transport electricity to homes and offices through power lines, we make sure it's high-voltage AC.

But many electronic devices, like computers and guitar amplifiers, require low voltage DC for most of their business. Therefore, they will contain a fairly large transformer to convert the 115 volts AC from your wall plug into 9 or 12-volt AC. Then they use a "diode" to convert this to DC they can use. Together with other components to stabilize the current, this part of a device is called its "power supply." The big transformer is easy to spot.

In a perfect universe, transformers would be completely efficient and we could step up voltages all day long, then step them down again all night, depending on our mood. There are, unfortunately, some obstacles to this plan.

First we have to overcome the opposition of self-inductance. At low frequencies (American power companies sell 60-cycle AC, which is considered a very low frequency), this is no problem. Then there is the resistance of the wire itself. A coil with many turns is a very long wire, and long wires have resistance. Wire is commonly made out of copper, so the loss in efficiency caused by the wire's resistance is called a "copper loss." This energy disappears from the circuit as it is converted to heat and radiates away from the transformer.

Another problem is that iron itself is a conductor and you know what that means: As the lines of magnetic force move through it, they are going to induce current in the core. These stray, disorganized currents are called "eddy currents." Any energy used to induce eddy currents is lost to the main current, and is effectively wasted. Since iron has a lot of resistance, these little currents within the core also contribute to the heat. To reduce eddy currents, iron cores are commonly made of many thin sheets of iron separated by thin insulators. You still get eddy currents, but they can't go very far.

Finally we have to overcome the tendency of the iron to stay magnetized. Every time the AC reverses direction, its magnetic polarity also reverses. Each particle of iron in the core acts like a tiny magnet, and a certain amount of energy is used to change the little north poles into little south poles. The faster you try to reverse them, the more they hate it, finally becoming hysterical and refusing to cooperate. They can only change so fast, after all. I guess this is why a magnet's resistance to a change in polarity is called "hysteresis." Part of the inefficiency in a transformer is because of the energy required to overcome hysteresis.

Taken together, hysteresis and eddy currents are called "iron losses." Every iron core transformer has both iron losses and copper losses. Most of the lost energy is converted to heat. As a result, transformers can get very hot. Do not try to pick up a large working transformer unless you want its manufacturer's name branded on your fingers.

A Brief Note From the Author

I hope the reader appreciates this author's self-restraint: I did not introduce a character named "Eddy Current" into the section on transformers. I just wanted to let you know that this omission was the result of a conscious decision, and not because it never occurred to me. The temptation was there, but I chose to maintain my path on the literary high ground. Even though I had a couple of good ideas for old Eddy, including a description, life history, psychological justifications for his motorcycle passion, and even a theme song for the TV series he might have inspired, I resisted.

I just wanted you to know.

Norwegian Nose Tricks

The folks who brought us "The Cheeseburger and the Tiger" have got you again. You are locked in a small white cell. The room is soundproof and padded, locked tight and heavily guarded. Escape seems unlikely. You know that your friend, professor Erik Heyerdahlson, a certified genius if there ever was one, is also a prisoner. In fact, he's being held in the next cell. If anyone can figure out a way to escape, it's professor Heyerdahlson. However, there is no way for you to communicate with him.

The only resource you've got is the same cardboard box filled with electrical components, and, of course, the two wires coming out of the wall that you now know are hooked up to an AC voltage source.

Every week or so all the prisoners are herded off to the prison locker room for a gang-shower. However, they are guarded closely. Any attempt to speak to another prisoner or communicate in any way is punished severely, usually by forcing the prisoner to do painful and embarrassing calisthenics.

While you're in the shower, you watch the professor out of the corner of your eye, wishing you could talk, even for a minute, and noticing how pitifully out of shape the old guy has let himself get.

The soap must bother him, you think, because he keeps wiggling his nose. Sniff, sniff... sniff, sniff, sniff. Suddenly you realize that this is not random sniffling. It's nose Morse code! You watch carefully, for there is little time. The professor sniffs out two words; "Mutual inductance..." Then the guards signal the end of the shower and everyone's herded back to their cell.

"Mutual inductance," you mutter to yourself in puzzlement. You know what it is, of course. It's magnetic coupling, like in a transformer. But how in the world can you use it now?

You dump the box of components on the floor and sort through them, hoping an idea will come to you. You have several little light bulbs. You could build a flasher for Morse code, but, of course, the professor wouldn't be able to see it through the concrete wall. Then you realize that he's probably got a box of components, too. If you could drill a hole through the wall, you could slip two wires through it. He could hook a light bulb up on his end, you could put a switch on yours. By turning the switch on and off in your cell you could make the light in his cell flash on and off. Then you could reverse the whole thing, put a light on your side and he could communicate with you! You have a switch, you have lots of wire, you've got a source of voltage. In a frenzy of excitement, you search through your components for something that you could use as a drill.

No dice. Your captors may not be the brightest guys in the world, but they're not codfish, either. There will be peace in the Middle East before you'll be able to scratch a hole through that concrete with carbon resistors and plastic capacitors. You sit back, disappointed, and start over.

Mutual inductance. That's what the professor had spelled out with his nose. At least, you think that's what he spelled out. But what did it mean? How could mutual inductance help you communicate?

Almost absent-mindedly you assemble some components that you might use in a mutual inductance experiment. There's a round oatmeal box, of course, and some wire. You coil the wire around the oatmeal box several times. No trumpets of revelation sound in your brain. The light seemed a good idea, you think. You've got a bulb that doesn't have too much resistance. Still without any real plan, you connect the two ends of your oatmeal-box coil to your light bulb. "Let's see," you say to yourself. "If I had another coil near this one, that was connected to alternating current, it would probably induce a current in this coil, and my light would go on." You draw a schematic of your little device:

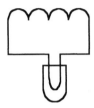

You shake your head, unable to figure out the puzzle. You set the whole works on the floor near the wall and stare at it, unwilling to admit defeat, but without any more ideas.

Suddenly, the light bulb flashes on, then quickly goes off again. You sit up, astonished. Was it your imagination, you wonder? That light bulb isn't hooked up to any electricity, just to a coil, yet you could swear it flashed on. You stare at it. Nothing happens.

Then it flashes on again, then off, in a pattern. It's Morse code! The professor must have made a similar coil in his room and hooked it to alternating current! Every time he turns the switch on, current flows through his coil. The magnetic field leaps outward from that coil and shrinks back to nothing 120 times per second, because it's 60-cycle AC. By dumb luck you have placed your coil very near his, on opposite sides of the concrete wall. That magnetic field doesn't care beans about concrete walls. It goes through easily and induces a current in your coil. The current lights your bulb.

You are very happy for two reasons. First, you have developed a way to communicate with the professor, which means that you now have access to his incredible brainpower and will probably come up with a way to escape.

Second, you have invented radio.

Radio:
Will It Ever Get Off the Ground?

"You mean that radio is just mutual inductance?" I asked.

"Right on, bro'" Mike responded. An early snowstorm was pelting the cabin with huge, wet flakes. Luckily, we had lots of firewood and hot chocolate. The fireplace blazed away as cheerful and warm as a Utah ski area operator; both were dancing tonight. Mike was plunking in a rather random fashion on an old ukulele that some previous occupant had left behind. He was determined to learn to play it before he went home.

"But there's music on radio, not light bulbs," I said.

Mike laughed.

"Low and slow, bro', one step at a time." He plunked a few more notes. I could tell he thought he was improving on "the old uke," as he called it. If so, it was a very subtle improvement. I was grateful when he put the old uke down.

"There's a couple of problems with the professor's radio," Mike said. "First, as you saw right away, there's no way to hear music or Morse code, even if the professor could send, or 'transmit' it. So we replace the light bulb with a speaker. Now we're ready."

"The next problem is that you can't transmit over long distances. You'd be lucky to get a message across a room."

"That might make it tough to sell advertising spots on your station," I said.

Mike grinned and poked at the fire. "There's a solution to that one."

"I figured there was."

"It turns out that, at higher frequencies, the lines of force travel further. If you coax the AC up to 500,000 cycles or more, it will go a heck of a lot further. Like miles."

I thought about that, and it didn't seem practical.

"I see two problems right away," I said. "How are we going to produce current that alternates that fast?"

"There is a way," Mike said, rather mysteriously.

"In a later chapter?"

"Bingo, bucko. What's your other problem?"

"Hysteresis. You'll never get the electromagnet in a speaker to change polarity that fast. It won't even get started before it has to switch."

"Groovy!" he said. "That's exactly the problem. It's why radio wasn't invented a hundred years earlier than it was. First they had to figure out how to produce high frequency AC, so it would travel great distances. But even if they could do that they couldn't change the induced current in their receiver into sound without using an electromagnet. Even the best electromagnet can't keep up with frequencies over 20,000 cycles or so. Can't even start to keep up. Kind of a tough problem."

"It sounds impossible to me."

"That's why they turned the Norwegians loose on it. For right now, all you have to remember is that radio is just mutual inductance, at high frequencies, usually across some distance. But you won't be ready to build a set until you learn about a couple more components."

I like puzzles, but this one was beyond me. Somehow it's possible to create current that alternates at more than a half million cycles. The lines of force that spread away from that current will travel for miles, carrying music and even television pictures along with them somehow. When they encounter another wire, they will induce a current in it that will resemble the current in the wire that caused them.

But to get any work out of electricity we usually have to change it into heat or magnetism. Probably not heat in this case. And a magnet can't reverse polarity quickly enough to respond to this high frequency. Hmm.

Think about it.

The Vacuum Tube Diode: A Pickle Jar With a Purpose

By now you can probably see a strange phrase like "vacuum tube diode" without breaking into a cold sweat. You recognize the game and know it's just like anything else: The more you practice making your jargon frightening and complex, the better you're going to be at it. Just listen to your CB radio on any Midwestern interstate if you want to hear simple thoughts transformed by jargon into long and important sounding conversations. American truck drivers are a national treasury of jargon. After listening to them for a while, electronics will sound easy to you again.

But perhaps I've strayed from my story.

When electrical people say "tube," they mean a sealed hollow tube, like a test tube. A pickle jar would work as a tube, if you could seal it very tight. When you put some electrical gizmo inside the tube, you call that thing an "element." We've already talked about one tube: a light bulb. The tiny tungsten filament is the only "element" in that tube. Most light bulbs are nitrogen tubes; instead of being filled with generic air, which has oxygen in it, they are filled with nitrogen, which is the next cheapest thing.

Nearly every kind of tube is a modified light bulb. They simply have other elements that interact with the basic filament.

If you pump the air out of a sealed pickle jar, you have created a vacuum or "absence of air." You and I know there will still be Greenie air in there, of course, but we won't tell a lot of people about that, will we? Greenie air was once known as "ether" by scientists who thought magnetism and light needed a medium, like water waves need water. The ether guys were ridiculed for a while, then came into favor and ridiculed the anti-ether guys, then it reversed again. No one talks about Greenie air or ether these days. It's just not worth the fight.

A "vacuum pickle jar" (or "vacuum tube," as it is commonly called) is fragile. The pressure of the outside air, no longer balanced by internal air, tends to crush vacuum tubes explosively if you're not careful. The picture tube in your television set may be a large vacuum tube. The violent "implosion" of a picture tube will shoot a thousand shards of glass into your body, creating large, painful, and hard-to-explain holes. People have been killed with this weapon. Do not play catch with vacuum tubes of any kind.

All by itself, a sealed pickle jar without any air inside isn't good for much. Sure, you can put a label on it that says, "Homemade Vacuum Tube," and show it to your friends. However, they may be skeptical. They may think it's still filled with air. "Prove it!" they will say tauntingly, and you will hang your head in despair. You can't tell a vacuum just by looking at it. If you don't think quickly, your friends will ridicule you and leave.

It was for this reason that scientists began experimenting with putting things inside the vacuum tube. There had to be some way of proving to their friends they had actually stored up a bunch of vacuum inside a jar.

Poor old Thomas Alva had this problem. He put a beetle in his pickle jar. When it died of lack of oxygen, his friends suspected he actually had poisoned the little fellow. They were a tough, cynical crowd, but Tom was persistent. He put his bamboo filament in a vacuum and it didn't burn up, but glowed for a long time. Still they were not convinced.

"Sure, it's a vacuum, Tom," they scoffed. "We won't fall for that old trick! You put nitrogen in there, just like last time. Everyone knows there's no such thing as a vacuum!"

"Hmm," said Tom, scratching his chin. His friends laughed and went out to play cribbage.

Thomas was not daunted. He was proud of his "Bamboo Filament-Vacuum-Pickle-Jar-Aquarium-Light." As was his style, he kept working on improving it, trying this and that. No one knew much about electronics back then (the electron theory had not yet been fabricated), and everything was hit and miss. Who would have guessed that bamboo would be a better filament than horse hair or tinsel? You just had to try anything you could think of and see what happened.

One of the things he tried was simply putting a piece of metal foil inside the jar, not touching the filament. This metal had a wire leading out of the jar so he could hook it to his battery. He hoped that it might have some affect on the filament.

As it turns out, it had absolutely no effect. However, in playing around with the wires he discovered, to his amazement, that a current would actually flow through the space between the hot filament and the metal foil! He knew that air was too good an insulator to allow that to happen, but a vacuum has much less resistance.

136

"Eureka!" he shouted, "A vacuum tube diode!" Then he ran off to get his buddies. Skeptically but dutifully, they filed back into his laboratory. He hooked it up, but nothing happened. His friends snickered.

"Honest, guys, it worked just a minute ago! Wait! Don't leave! There must be a loose connection here some place..." Frantically he jiggled the wires, but to no avail. The filament glowed, the battery was good, but no current would flow through the space between the filament and the piece of metal.

"I'll give you jellybeans if you stay!" he shouted but they were already out the door, laughing and shaking their heads.

"Poor old Thomas Alva," they said to each other. "Dreaming again. I'm afraid he'll never amount to much."

"He only does these things because no one will give him a real job."

"Sad, very sad. I hope he grows up soon."

It was probably in the middle of the night when the solution came to Thomas. He went downstairs, still in his underwear, excitedly popped some jellybeans into his mouth, and reversed the wires.

It worked! Current flowed from the filament to the metal foil, but it wouldn't flow backward, from the foil to the filament. He must have hooked it up backward when his friends were watching.

He had invented a sort of one-way valve for electricity. Because it had two elements it has come to be known as a diode (which means "two elements"). Unfortunately, he didn't see any use for it at the time, and he didn't want to embarrass his friends by showing them how foolish they were, so he made a note about it, went back to bed, and forgot about it. The little sheet of metal became known as the plate. I believe this is because you could make it out of aluminum foil, which is often used at picnics to hold potato salad and beans while you eat them, when someone forgets to bring the paper plates. In this case, the jargon is inescapably logical. A diode has two elements: a filament and a plate.

Everyone knows that Tom discovered the vacuum tube diode, but since he dropped the ball, he isn't given much credit. Years later, a Norwegian fellow named Fleming patented the thing and made the money. Thomas Alva was well-versed in Ohm's law, however, at least the part about naming things. He declared the phenomenon of electricity flowing through a vacuum from a hot filament to a cold plate the "Edison Effect," and it's been called that ever since.

This is the symbol for the vacuum tube diode:

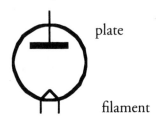

plate

filament

Barefoot Greenies, Dancin' in the Moonlight

"It's not a lie," I explained to Mike. "It's a dramatization."

"Did Edison eat jelly beans?" Mike fumed, his face turning even greener.

"Well, shoot, I bet if he had them..."

"You don't know that, man! You made the whole thing up! Did he sleep in his underwear?"

"Everybody sleeps in their underwear."

"Maybe in Norway they do! Edison might have been a pajama kind of guy! In fact, I bet he was. How can you expect people to take your book seriously if you keep making up these little stories?"

"I was just trying to make it interesting."

"Electronics is not supposed to be interesting, man! If it was interesting, everybody would understand it."

"I'm sorry."

"It's Okay I just think you ought to stay a little closer to the truth."

"You mean, more Greenies and less Edison?"

"Exactly. You don't want to confuse people."

"I'll try to do better."

He took a couple of deep breaths and calmed himself down. "I think you ought to go over vacuum tube diodes again," he said.

I thought for a minute. I had to handle this carefully.

"How would you explain them?" I asked cautiously. His face brightened and began to fade to a more normal lettuce-green.

"A filament is a blacktop road, at noon, on a hot summer day," he said. "And all the Greenies are barefoot. The metal plate is a big expanse of cool, shady grass. It doesn't take much of a party to convince us to step off the pavement. On the other hand, it will take a lot of beer, beautiful women, and a big-name rock group playing for free to convince us to leave the shady grass and abuse our little green feet on that filament."

"That's a pretty good analogy," I said slowly.

"Analogy my green foot!" he yelled. "It's what goes on! I've there, man. This isn't jellybeans and pickle jars! This is truth!"

"I meant it was easy to understand." Mike seemed pretty touchy today. I guessed he was homesick. "Want to hear something funny?" I said.

"Always, man, always."

"Well, would you like to hear how they explain a vacuum tube diode in the electron theory?"

"Sock it to me." Electron theory stories always seemed to cheer him up, the way the Mickey Mouse Club had cheered me up after school when I was a kid.

"The heat of the filament 'boils off' a little cloud of electrons that hovers around it. They call it a 'space charge.' Of course the space charge, being loose electrons, has a negative charge. Any electrons that try to get to the filament from the plate are repelled by that negative charge. But if the current is going the other direction, the electrons in the space charge fly off that cloud and move toward the plate easily, attracted to its positive charge."

Mike was chuckling. The electron theory never stopped amazing him.

"To improve a diode," I continued, "they often surround the filament with some material that boils off more electrons. They call whatever is boiling off electrons the cathode, and the filament just heats it."

Mike was actually laughing now.

"An artificially heated black-top road," he said. "What a groove! So you can burn your feet even if the sun's not shining."

"Anyway," I continued, "current will flow from the cathode to the plate, but not backward. The vacuum tube diode is a one-way valve for electricity."

"Thanks, man," Mike said. "I feel a lot better now."

So What?

"Okay, Kenn," I hear you saying. "So what? Why would anybody want a vacuum tube diode? A one-way valve. Bah! Humbug! Another useless invention!"

Well, of course, that's what they said about Silly Putty, too. Great stuff, everybody said, but what's it good for?

Maybe that's a bad example. The person who comes up with a really great use for Silly Putty will make some money. Think of a military application and you'll make a fortune. But perhaps I have strayed from my story.

Somebody already came up with a use for a diode, and a name for that use. It's called "rectifying." When you "rectify" something, that usually means you correct it. I rectify my spelling all the time; we all try to rectify our mistakes. In electricity, you rectify alternating current when you change it to direct current. I suppose Edison or his followers came up with the word because they thought direct current was right and alternating current was wrong. I don't know. Anyway, if you're in the mood to rectify some AC, you can do it with diodes.

Picture a diode, a one-way valve, in an AC circuit. When the current is headed "the right way" or "forward" through it, the diode will have no effect at all. It might as well be a wire. But when the current reverses directions, those Greenies will be faced with bad news. A space charge is in their way. The bridge is down, the road is closed. The current simply stops.

When the current reverses directions again, so it is once more headed "forward" through the diode, it can move easily. We're back in business, at least for a moment.

Current will only flow through this circuit for half of each cycle, only when it's heading the "right" direction. An observer would think we were using direct current that came in little bursts, on then off. Pulses, you might say. We have used a diode to convert AC into "pulsating DC." We have "rectified" the AC.

Sure, we're only getting electricity to flow half the time, and we're wasting the other half. But then, we only pay the power company for the current that actually flows into our house, and if it's not flowing during the "off" part of each cycle it doesn't cost us anything. A rectifier that changes AC into pulsating DC is called a "half-wave rectifier."

I know, I know. You're way ahead of me. You've already figured out a way to use a half-wave rectifier. It solves a problem you've been worrying about since it came up in an earlier chapter. The guy who originally solved that problem, incidentally, made a bunch of money, and he didn't have any more information than you do now.

You should be proud of yourself.

Another Look at Radio:
Was Marconi Secretly Norwegian?

The fog rolled like a huge cotton steamroller across the North Sea, blundering silently up a lonely fiord, hurrying the evening ahead of it. In the deepening darkness, a lone man in a tiny boat rowed wearily toward the warm yellow glow of a cottage window, its light a faint beacon in the pine trees above the water. He was exhausted, but he knew the fog would soon obliterate that light, his only landmark. Without it, he would quickly become lost in the cold Norwegian night, at the mercy of the freezing tide and the Arctic fog. He lowered his head, and kept on rowing.

Finally he reached the tiny landing and tied up the boat. With his last bit of strength he stumbled up the path to the cottage. In the dim light, he could make out the crudely painted name on the mailbox, "Alexander Graham Amdahl," and for the first time, he smiled. He had made it.

The door opened before him, he stumbled through and collapsed on the wooden floor.

"Sven! " The old woman cried. "Papa, it's Sven! Put on some more lutefisk' Are you all right, Sven?"

"Ah, Ma," groaned the young man as she helped him to his feet. "How many times do I have to tell you not to call me Sven anymore? It's Marconi. Gugliameli Marconi."

The old woman sniffed. "You'll always be my little Sven. I don't know why you're ashamed of your heritage, anyway. There have been a lot of great Norwegians."

Sven sat in a chair. This happened every time he came home.

"There is no demand for Norwegian scientists, Ma. These days you have to be Italian, or at least American. It's just the way it is, Ma. Scientists have to have stage names, just like actors."

"Ya, sure, you betcha!" She exaggerated her accent. "Papa, wake up!" she yelled. "Our son Marconi is here! Throw away the good fish and put on some noodles! Ya, sure, he eats only noodles now."

"Ah, Ma, I can't help the way it is."

"And what about Leif Erikson? Wasn't he a great Norwegian?"

"You know what they say about him? They say he found America, all right, but couldn't think of anything to do with it. That's what they say."

"Sven! When did you get here?" An old man shuffled into the room rubbing his eyes and pushing his long red beard away from his nose and mouth.

"Hi, Pop. I didn't mean to wake you."

"Just resting my eyes, son. The lutefisk is about done, by the smell. Will you stay for dinner?"

"Pop, it's 50 miles to the nearest town, against the current, and I'm alone in a rowboat."

The old man stared at him blankly.

"Yeah, Pop, I'll stay for dinner. Thanks."

The old man's face brightened, as an idea bubbled to the surface of his mind.

"I have some grog in the barn," he whispered, winking mischievously at Sven. Sven just nodded. When his wife wasn't looking, the old man eased out the door.

"So, Sven, it's been almost a year. You must have another electrical problem for your father."

"Gee whiz, Ma, can't a guy just come home for a nice visit with his parents without you thinking he wants something?"

"Is it in the little bag there?"

Sven started to protest further, then stopped, and simply nodded. "Yeah, Ma, it's in the bag."

It was later, when the potatoes and fish had been cleared away from the table, and Sven and his father were drinking a second cup of hot grog, that Sven pulled the little devices from his bag.

"More toys, Sven?" The old man became suddenly interested.

"Yeah, Pop. Two different things. This one's a buzzer."

"Ya, sure, Sven, I can see it's a buzzer. You got your electromagnet and your little strip of metal. Turn on the 'uice, the magnet pulls on the strip of metal. Turn off the 'uice, the metal springs back. On and off, on and off. Click, click, click. Pretty soon the little thing is a'buzzin' back and forth."

"That's right, Pop. A buzzer is just an electromagnet and a strip of metal. The strip of metal is arranged so it's also a switch that turns the magnet on and off each time it moves."

"Well, Sven, dot vas an easy problem, ya! Shall we have some more grog?"

"No, Pop, that's not the problem. But I guess I could take just a little more grog. If you are, that is. Just a sip." They both filled their cups to the brim with the hot fruit liquor. Then Sven took out two large coils of wire and set them on the table.

"Ya, sure, Sven, now you got coils."

"Right, Pop. And if I set them close together like this, they act like a transformer."

"You mean the 'uice inde first one der induces some 'uice in de udder one der?" His accent became more pronounced the more grog he drank.

"Ya, sure, I mean, right Pop. And the two coils don't touch each other. There's a space between them. The only thing that connects them in any way is the lines of force, the magnetism produced by the first coil. See, I have this idea that those lines of force are the key. I think they act kind of like waves. Electrical waves, or magnetic waves. I can't make up my mind which. Right now I call them electromagnetic waves."

"You call magnetic lines of force electromagnetic waves?"

"Yeah, if they're moving I do. Anyway, here's the problem: What if I hook my battery up to the first coil, and my buzzer to the second coil?"

"Yumpin' yimminy! You got a buzzer that's a'buzzin' that's not hooked up to a battery! You'll make a fortune!"

"No, Pop, it's not that simple. First, the coils only work with current that is constantly changing, like AC current. A battery won't work."

"You mean because of Bruce the Duck?"

Sven shook his head. "That's just a fairy tale, Pop. Nobody believes in little green Norwegian ducks." The old man looked disappointed, but he didn't argue. "It's the lines of magnetic force, Pop, the electromagnetic waves. You know that."

"Ya, I forgot."

"My problem is that the magnetic lines travel a lot farther if the current is changing directions very fast."

"Und why would that be?"

"I don't know, Pop, I just discovered it. But it's like this: Magnetic lines of force, or electromagnetic waves, at slow frequencies act like big old beach balls. They can knock you down but you can't throw 'em very far. Very fast frequencies are more like sling-shot pellets; with the same amount of power they'll travel a long distance and go right through your volleyball net, but they don't make near as big a splash if they land in the water."

"Dot makes sense."

"So, if I use a very high frequency, I can get the electromagnetic waves to travel pretty far. At least I think I can. But the magnet in my buzzer takes some time to magnetize and demagnetize. And the coil

144

around it has a lot of self-induction, so it resists any change in current. By the time I increase the frequency enough for these waves to travel very far, it's way too fast for my electromagnet. There isn't time to overcome self induction and magnetize the iron core before the current is going the other direction. So my buzzer just sits there."

"Dot's a problem, sure."

"But if I can figure out some way to solve that problem, boy, then we'd really have something. A wireless buzzer! If you can figure it out, I'll, I'll…" He searched around for some suitable incentive. "I'll name it after your old hunting dog!"

"You'd do that, Sven?" The old man was clearly moved. "You'd name it after old Radio?"

"You bet, Pop."

"Dot would be something! I can see it now: a wireless buzzer! You could send messages across town without wires! Maybe across the country! Oofta! Maybe you could figger out a way to send voices, maybe even music, from country to country! Maybe there's a way to send pictures with your wireless buzzer! Maybe…"

Sven stopped him. "Don't be stupid, Pop. That's the grog talking. None of that is possible. But think of this: Maybe you could make little buzzers that doctors and other important people could carry around with them. Then, when it was their turn to tee off, the golf course could just buzz them. Now, that's the practical application. Every doctor in the world will want one."

The old man let out a long, slow whistle of approval. "Ya, sure, I got to hand it to you on dot one. If you figger it out, you're a rich one for sure. Good luck, Sven."

"Marconi, Pop, remember? Call me Marconi."

Isn't It Good:
A Norwegian Probably Would

The next morning Sven got up before sunrise. Being careful not to wake his parents, he put on a jacket and walked toward the water's edge. The deep fjord was nearly black against the smoky green of the forested hills. The earliest of birds were beginning to sing, and there were still a few faint stars visible in the awakening sky. The mist was light, for Norway, and it moved like a slow dance of ghosts over everything.

Sven hadn't slept well. The solution to his problem seemed tantalizingly close, yet somehow he couldn't find it. Whenever he was hopelessly stumped like this, Sven returned to his magical homeland. The cold water and green mountains always seemed to know the answer.

He went over the problem again and again. High-frequency electromagnetic waves travel far, but electromagnets can't respond to high frequency. Electromagnets respond to direct current or slowly changing AC, but those didn't travel very far. It was a paradox. And, of course, no one had even proved conclusively that electromagnetic waves existed.

Sven sat on a rock at the water's edge. The fjord was calm, looking like a long, glassy snake winding through the forested cliffs. Through the mist, he saw a single rowboat moving toward the opposite shore. When it reached the shallow water it casually turned and headed back across. After several minutes, it reached the near shore and turned around once more. Sven guessed it was a fisherman crisscrossing the water to improve his odds of passing a fish.

"It looks like my electromagnet," he thought. "It changes directions so painfully slowly." He smiled at the analogy. "Click," he said, as it reached one shore and slowly turned toward the other. Several minutes later, as it finished another crossing, Sven said "click" once more.

The boat was gradually moving closer to Sven. He could see the wet oars rising out of the water rhythmically, and became entranced with their motion. Up and down, up and down. Something about the oars, he thought...

He was so preoccupied with staring at the oars, as if somehow they held the answer to his problem, that he didn't look up at the boat's occupant until it nearly ran into him.

"Hi," said a soft and feminine voice. It was a beautiful blonde girl, perhaps 18 years old, smiling shyly at him from the boat. She had a fabulous tan, which was especially noticeable because she wasn't wearing a stitch of clothing. She radiated the healthy glow of someone who rows a boat across a fjord every morning, probably right after her sauna.

"Hello," Sven answered. "How's the fishing?" The girl giggled, then answered in Norwegian.

"It depends on what you're fishing for."

Sven noticed then that she didn't have a pole, and felt a little silly.

"Would you like to come in my little boat?" she asked sweetly.

"What?"

"Isn't it good?" She pointed to her wooden rowboat. Sven forced himself to look at the boat. It was, indeed, a fine little craft. "There is a little cove not far from here where the fisherman say they have very good luck." She smiled again and pushed her long blonde hair out of her eyes. "You can row, if you want."

"Eureka!" Sven shrieked. "That's it!" He raced back up the hill toward his parents' cottage, leaving the girl staring at him in amazement.

"Another time," he yelled over his shoulder. "Thanks!"

"It was nothing," she said to herself as he disappeared into the trees. She shrugged and turned her little boat back toward the deep water.

Things like that happen in Norway.

An Old Hunting Dog is Immortalized

"The signal is like oars!" Sven burst through the cottage door.

"Who was that fellow in the boat?"

"I don't know, Ma." Sven waved that subject aside impatiently. "Listen, I've got the answer to my wireless buzzer!"

"Are you up, Sven?" His father appeared in the doorway.

"Yeah, Pop, I think I've got the answer! Or at least part of it!"

"Ya, sure, that's swell, Sven. Mama, I need some coffee." The old man sat down at the table, holding his head with both hands.

"See, the alternating current is like oars, going back and forth very quickly."

147

"Where's that coffee, Mama?"

"Now listen to me, Pop! The current in my receiver is going back and forth, just like oars. But the boat won't move if I never take the oars out of the water! And my buzzer won't work unless I eliminate half the impulses! I only want to let half of the electricity through to my electromagnet, just the pulses that are all going the same direction. That way, the iron core never has to reverse polarity. I need some sort of one-way valve for electricity. Then my lines of force will act like oars pushing a boat. When they're moving the wrong direction, I'll pull them out of the water. But what could I use?"

His father took a noisy sip of coffee, sucking in about as much air as liquid.

"I suppose you could use a vacuum tube diode," the old man said quietly. Sven stared in amazement. Of course. That would do it. Then he reached under the table to scratch the scruffy hunting dog behind the ears.

"Radio, old boy," he said. "This is your lucky day."

Cat's Whisker Diode

It was not until the next day that Gugliameli Marconi, with a profound sense of disappointment, realized that the vacuum tube diode had not yet been invented. A lesser man might have been crushed, but not this proud Norwegian. He set out to invent it.

In that venture, he also failed. He did discover that a jar filled with iron filings would conduct electricity in the presence of radio waves and would not conduct without them. He called his device a "coherer." The device itself has faded into oblivion without descendants, except for plates that get hot in microwave ovens. With it, however, Marconi proved the existence of radio waves. A fellow named Nikola Tesla also proved it, and in fact proved it earlier. When the matter of, "Who did, in fact, discover radio?" went to court, Tesla won. This fact has not stopped generations of science teachers from misleading their students. If you want the good grade, lie and say that Marconi discovered radio.

Practically speaking, radio became possible with the invention of the "cat's whisker diode." As you might guess, it is an odd little fellow, but it did change the world, and its descendants are the brains within modern computers. The "cat's whisker diode" may be worth a moment of our time.

Some crystals have an interesting property. If you squeeze them, they act like a tiny battery and produce voltage. A normal battery converts chemical energy into electricity. These little crystals convert physical pressure into electricity. This is called the "piezoelectric effect." Don't try to pronounce it. It can't be done. These crystals have too much resistance to be considered good conductors. On the other hand, they don't have enough resistance to be good insulators. They fall in between good conductors and good insulators in a category called "semiconductors."

If we gently push the point of a needle against one of these crystals, we create a voltage in the tiny area surrounding our little weapon. It's as if Greenies move away from the pain, the way a crowd of people would move away from a crazy fireman in the park who is spraying water from a fire hose. The needle is surrounded by a negative "space charge," just as our lunatic fireman is surrounded by a circle of people, just out of range.

Without the fireman, people would walk easily through the park in any direction. Now, however, they avoid the big wet circle.

In the same way, electricity going through our crystal will now avoid the point of the needle. In fact, electricity won't flow in a circuit if it has to travel from the crystal to the needle. The negative space charge prevents it.

On the other hand, electricity will flow from the needle to the crystal.

Imagine there's a manhole near our fire-hose-swinging friend, and a bunch of people are down there, trying to get out. As soon as one climbs out, he sees the fireman and makes a mad dash for the crowd. It's his only choice; by now the next person is already halfway out of the manhole, and if he stands still, he'll be drenched. People can move from the manhole toward the crowd, but it will take some pretty special motivation to convince them to fight their way through the crowd, toward the wet circle and toward the manhole. Especially if they're in their good clothes.

Which is just my way of saying that electricity will flow only in one direction through our little device. It will flow from the needle to the crystal, but not the reverse.

In the early days of electronics, the needle was held in place by a spring. Then it was replaced with a single piece of sharp, springy wire which pressed into the crystal because of its own tension. This wire was curved, like a cat's whisker, and the device became known as a "cat's whisker diode." It was simple, it was cheap, and it worked like magic. For the first half of the 20th century, the cat's whisker diode was a big deal. All over the world, people used them to make little radio receivers called "crystal sets." Many people who propelled the world into 21st century electronics were first enchanted and hooked by building a crystal set.

Any long wire would serve as an antenna; distant radio transmitters induced an alternating current in it. The diode rectified this AC, turned it into pulsating DC. This was called "detecting" the signal, and the diode was the "detector." Now the little magnet in a speaker or headphone didn't have to change polarity, and it could keep up with the signal. You had a radio receiver.

There are other ways to make diodes, and other uses for them too. The symbol for a diode is this:

This symbol represents Greenies, in their little cars, slamming into a brick wall. Current can't flow in the direction the arrow is pointing, but it can flow the opposite direction. Actually, the symbol was designed in the days when conventional current was accepted as truth. "Conventional current" sounds sort of familiar to you, doesn't it, yet you can't quite remember what I'm talking about. It doesn't matter. The symbol shows Greenies slamming into a brick wall when they try to go the wrong direction.

150

The development of diodes and radio caused electrical jargonists to shift gears. As long as we were only talking about circuits involving switches, resistance, and magnetism (like house wiring, lights, and motors), we were studying "electricity." Guys that wire houses and fix refrigerator motors are "electricians," which means "technicians of electricity." Once we added vacuum tubes, crystal sets, and electro-magnetic waves, the simple electrical picture stories became less satisfying. How do you explain a vacuum tube diode if electricity is like water flowing through a pipe? You can't. That's the reason that the electron theory was able to hijack science and force it to fly to Jamaica. Teachers needed "space charges" and the "piezoelectric effect" to explain what was going on inside the devices that every 12-year-old kid in America was building. The electron theory, and the study of "electronics" was hatched. This theory and new jargon had the added benefit of spoiling the fun. How many 12-year-old kids do you know today who can build and understand their own radios? They have been spared all the adventures that their interest might have led them upon. We have developed effective tools to nip their natural curiosity in the bud, before it can develop into a life-long passion. Just put "piezoelectric effect" on the test, and take off points for spelling.

When we study vacuum tube diodes, crystal diodes, radio, or any of their descendants, we are studying electronics, rather than electricity. "Electronics" is the study of alleged electrons and circuits that employ them, circuits that involve capacitance, inductance, space charges, semi-conductors, and electromagnetic waves. If it's not like water flowing through a pipe, it's electronics.

Of course, we're missing one final bit of jargon. If the study of electrons is "electronics" and the study of current in simple circuits is "electricity," what do we call the study of Greenies?

That's simple. We call it, "Man's Never-Ending Quest For Truth."

The Crystal Set

An antenna is just a long wire or other conductor. Of course, it has its own symbol:

A simple speaker consists of an electromagnet pulling against some metal foil. The strength of the current determines how strongly it will pull. As the current changes, the magnet pulls the foil, then relaxes a bit, and we hear sound. The smaller the magnet, the less current it will require. Headphones have little speakers inside them. The symbol for headphones is:

And here's the symbol for a speaker:

Put them together and you get a crystal set, the simplest radio receiver:

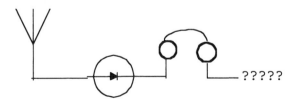

The diode can be solid state or vacuum or cat's whisker, and you can buy one for less than the cost of a cup of coffee. If you had time to fool around with various crystals and springs, with luck, you could even build one yourself. Some people have metal fillings in their teeth that act as diodes and therefore as detectors – they actually hear radio stations in their skulls. Dentists have had to choose different materials for fillings just so their patients don't go crazy. Unfortunately, they didn't get to some of us in time.

The antenna will work best if it's a fairly long wire. Notice this: All the power for this receiver is coming from a distant radio station. There is no battery or other power source, only the current that is induced in your antenna by some anonymous transmitter, perhaps halfway around the world from you. Depending on how powerful the closest radio station is, you can now listen to it for free, forever.

We can improve the design a bit. Right now, there isn't really a complete circuit for Greenies. They move to the end of the line, then stop. If we add a big capacitor, they will keep moving until the plate is full. They'll be able to move through a longer part of each cycle:

Of course, about the biggest capacitor we have available is Mother Earth. We can park Greenies in the soil of North America for a long time before we fill up every nook and cranny. We let Greenies flow into the ground for part of each cycle, and through our headphones the other part. We have "grounded" the circuit. The symbol for grounding is:

Here is our improved crystal set:

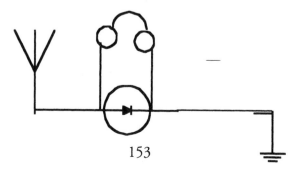

Now we have a dandy little radio. You may hear stations in other states or even other countries. However, if there is more than one strong station, you'll pick them all up. If you live far from any stations, and the weather isn't right, your reception will be faint or non-existent.

Both of those problems can be solved.

Filters

Filters are everywhere, and they all have this in common: they allow some things to pass through them while stopping other things. Coffee filters allow liquid coffee to pass through them but stop coffee grounds. The oil filter in your car lets oil pass through but stops bits of dirt. A fish net is a really a fish filter: It lets water through, but not fish.

When we talk about electrical filters, we really mean "frequency filters." They let some frequencies through, while stopping others.

A capacitor can be used as a filter. As you recall, direct current stops after an instant when it encounters a capacitor. A capacitor "filters out" direct current. Since higher frequencies are less affected by a capacitor than lower frequencies, a capacitor can be used to filter out those lower frequencies. Since a capacitor has little effect if the frequency is high enough, a capacitor is considered a "high pass" filter. It apparently allows high frequency to pass through, while stopping lower frequencies. Of course, no current actually passes through the dielectric.

A coil is another simple filter. Slow frequencies and direct current pass easily through a coil, while high frequencies are choked out. A coil is a "low pass" filter.

We could make our crystal set more selective by adding either a coil or a capacitor. If we added a capacitor, we might reduce that low hum that you hear when you receive radio signals from fluorescent lights. Because these are in the range of 60 cycles (a low frequency), a capacitor will stop them. If you add a coil, you might eliminate the high-frequency crackling static made by distant lightning and sparking electric motors. Either a coil or a capacitor would probably clean up the sound a bit, assuming the signal is strong enough to overcome this added resistance.

But you want it all, don't you? You don't want to listen to the neighbor's fluorescent lights or his garbage disposal. In fact, there's a couple of radio stations you'd just as soon eliminate while you're at it. The solution is to use capacitors and coils in combinations. Because both come in many sizes, we can make very specific filters.

If you put a capacitor and a coil in series with each other, the slowest frequencies will be opposed by the capacitor, and the fastest will be opposed by the coil. Only those frequencies somewhere in the middle will be able to get through. For any capacitor in series with any coil, one frequency will be best. This frequency, the one which encounters the least impedance is the "resonant" frequency. Higher and lower frequencies will encounter more impedance. If you pick your coil and capacitor carefully, you can "tune" your circuit so that the frequency used by your favorite radio station is the resonant frequency.

Something a little different happens when you put a coil and capacitor in parallel like this:

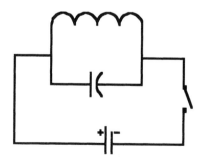

We have given our Greenies a choice of two routes. Very high frequencies will choose the capacitor route, and will encounter little opposition. Low frequencies and direct current will choose the coil route, and will also encounter little opposition.

But the middle frequencies will have trouble. They will be high enough so that the coil opposes them, yet low enough that the capacitor also opposes them. No matter which route our Greenies of intermediate frequencies take, they're going to run into opposition. For every specific combination of coil and capacitor, some frequency is really going to be in trouble. This intermediate frequency is fast enough that the coil will stop it, and yet slow enough that the capacitor will also stop it. That frequency is the resonant frequency for this type of circuit. With some skill, you could use this type of filter to eliminate the frequency of some particularly objectionable radio station. It's usually the station that either your parents or your children listen to all the time.

We will use this circuit again, so we must give it a name. It's called a "tank circuit," because Greenies at a certain frequency jump into one end, but they don't seem to jump out. They just swim around between the capacitor and the coil as if it were a water tank in the twilight zone.

We can add more coils and more capacitors to make our filters more sophisticated and expensive, but the principle is the same. There are formulas to predict exactly how any combination in series or parallel will behave.

The final refinement is this: We can replace one of the components in our filter (usually the capacitor) with a variable component (a variable capacitor). A variable component, as the name implies, is one whose value is adjustable. When you turn the knobs on your radio, you are really turning variable resistors and capacitors, to change the frequency of your filter, or the resistance in your volume control circuit. Variable components have the same symbol as their fixed counterparts, with an arrow through them.

When we turn the knob on the variable capacitor, we increase and decrease its capacitance. As we do this, the resonant frequency changes too. By using a coil and a variable capacitor, we can tune our radio to eliminate all frequencies except the one being produced by our favorite station.

A Radio Transmitter With No Parts

On the mysterious planet Earth, there is a naturally occurring radio that was broadcasting its message long before the dinosaurs mucked their way out of the swamp water. This transmitter still sends its lonely message across the face of the planet, as well as out into space, thousands of times each day. It is vastly more powerful than any transmitter humans have manufactured, yet is incredibly simple. Every electrical engineer knows about it; indeed, if they did not design protective circuits into radios, sooner or later its strength would destroy them all.

Yet we have never decoded it. In fact, we assume there is no message, for the signal is so powerful we can't imagine a technology that could actually control it. We prefer not to consider the possibility of a civilization with a transmitter on so grand a scale. Our teachers tell us about it only casually, perhaps because of their ignorance, perhaps because of their fear.

The transmitter is lightning.

During its brief transmission, enough current to power a small city is channeled between the earth and a cloud, or between two clouds, alternating at a million cycles per second or more. The radio waves it produces travel outward at close to the speed of light, inducing current in every conductor they encounter. If that conductor is your radio antenna, despite the filters, you will hear static. If the conductor is a power line, the added current they induce will travel through the wire as a power surge. This extra current will create heat in any resistance it encounters. It will melt fuses, light-bulb filaments, and computer components miles away from the lightning itself. At close range, so much current is induced in a "receiver" that the heat from resistance will melt iron pipe and vaporize heavy power cables.

It is a radio transmitter without parts or schematic. A human would receive the Nobel Prize if he could conceive of such a thing, design it, and place it into operation. Yet we think of lightning as no more than the interesting but inconsequential special effects of a rainstorm. Of course, that's because no message is being sent.

Or is there? Consider this: Perhaps we overlook lightning as evidence of visitors from outer space, simply because it seems so natural, so universal, so uncontrollable. What if, eons ago, earth were colonized by a race of beings so advanced they were able to use these bursts to communicate with their home planet? What if they're still here, an outpost of galactic explorers stationed secretly among us for the last million years, watching, listening, and reporting on our progress. We would never know about it, or decode their messages, because we're not listening.

And, of course, they may not want us to listen. They may find us primitive and uninteresting specimens. Easier to observe us if we think we're alone. If that's true, they may go out of their way to keep us from learning the truth. This is just something to think about.

Especially if you hear that I've been struck by lightning.

Spark Gap Transmitter

Lightning is just a big spark, of course. Given enough voltage, electricity will flash through the air. The lines of force this current creates will induce a huge surge of current headed "backward," which induces a third current headed "forward" and so on. All this self-induction happens very quickly. A spark contains a huge range of frequencies, from very slow to a million cycles per second or more. The air, because of its resistance, gets white hot and we see the spark or the lightning. This super-heated air expands violently and we hear a little snap, or thunder. Many of the lines of force escape as electromagnetic waves. Those that are at high frequencies travel for miles.

If we could make a machine that would create continuous sparks, we would have a sort of radio transmitter ourselves. That is exactly what the first transmitters were.

The trick to creating a spark is to develop a high voltage. Greenies must have a lot of motivation to leap into the void. We can use a step-up transformer to increase voltage, but we need constantly changing current to use a transformer. Early experimenters didn't have AC lines to their houses and laboratories. However, they could easily build DC batteries out of sulfuric acid and scraps of zinc or other metals and carbon. You know, stuff they had laying around the house. They used this DC to power "spark gap transmitters."

The spark gap transmitter is not much more than a buzzer. A buzzer consists of an electromagnet aimed at a piece of spring steel. The spring steel serves two functions. The sound it makes as it hits the magnet and springs back many times a second puts the "buzz" in a buzzer. The spring also acts as its own switch. When the magnet pulls the steel away from its contact, the circuit becomes open. The electromagnet turns itself off by pulling the steel switch open. Without that pull, the steel springs back, closing the switch and turning the magnet back on. I have had jobs like that myself.

Buzzer:

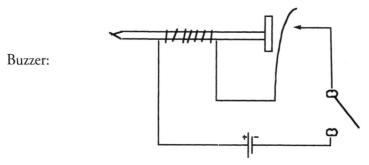

If you add a little rubber diaphram and a one-way air valve, you've got an aquarium pump to make bubbles for your fish. But we can do even more with a buzzer.

Each time the buzzer turns itself on, current builds for an instant, and lines of force grow. Each time it turns itself off, the lines of force shrink. Because these lines of force are constantly moving, we can use them to induce a secondary current.

The core of our electromagnet is a nail, but it could be any piece of iron. If we wrap the nail with a second coil of wire, having more turns than the first one, we have made a step-up transformer. If the secondary coil has 10 times as many loops, or turns, as the original electromagnet coil, and we use a 12-volt battery to power the device, we will discover 120 volts in the secondary. If we connect this output to the primary of still another step-up transformer, we can change it to over 1,000 volts. Now we're in sparking range.

Adding a capacitor to the circuit will provide a parking spot for Greenies that have been sent backward through the wire by self-induction, so they don't build up and leap across the switch and waste the energy we have invested in them. As the circuit becomes more attractive to them, they will rejoin it, adding their enthusiasm to the action. If we mount the two ends of our last secondary coil close together, we will see a series of nearly continuous sparks leap between them. Add a switch and we can turn the whole thing on and off. When it's on, sparks will fly, and you'll be transmitting radio waves. Turn off the switch, and the signal stops. If you know Morse code, you could send a message to your buddy across town, who would receive it on his crystal set. For less than it costs to buy lunch, you have your own radio station.

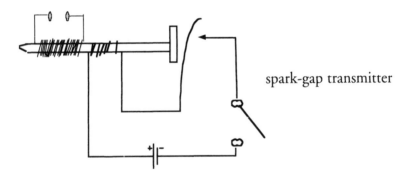

spark-gap transmitter

A word of caution: Although it's perfectly legal for me to tell you all this, and even legal for you to build one of these, it may not be legal for you to actually operate it. Depending on how much power you start with, and how you construct it, you may interfere with radio and television reception for some distance. You must have a license to operate radio transmitters, and you don't have one.

In fact, license laws became necessary around 1900 because so many people were sending out messages with these spark gap transmitters that ships at sea couldn't get emergency messages through all the radio "noise." Spark gaps have no frequency control. If you can't resist building one, use some common sense. Depending on your skill and luck you may mess up radios in Japan, South America, and Uranus. You could interfere with an airline pilot's communications and cause a real emergency. Incidentally, even the laws didn't put much of a dent in the enthusiasm of all the amateur radio operators ("hams"). Finally, they had to resort to jargon and the electron theory to steer people away from the hobby.

The folks who enforce the license laws do not have a sense of humor. You should be especially careful about building little projects until you understand enough electronics that you don't get caught. Until then, please don't leave this book anywhere near your experiments. I don't want to be considered an accomplice.

As I Was a'Modulatin' Over the Hill

Radio is like a corked bottle cast out into the ocean. It may travel for a great distance, but by itself it conveys little information. Early radio was a series of long and short bursts of radio waves sent as patterns in Morse code. This is sort of like stringing a bunch of bottles together with a pattern to their spacing. Although this method is still used sometimes, and you have to learn Morse code to get some radio licenses, we have also learned a couple of ways to put a message inside the bottle, using the radio wave itself as a carrier. We modify or "modulate" the radio waves to accomplish this.

Some microphones are variable resistors whose resistance changes in exact proportion to the sound waves that strike them. If a microphone is in your transmitting circuit, the current will vary in strength right along with the sound, and so will the radio waves produced. We have changed the plain radio waves – "modulated" their intensity, or their "amplitude." This is called "amplitude modulation" and is commonly known as "AM radio." Our receiver will filter out all the unmodulated carrier wave, our detector will rectify the alternating current, and we will be left with nothing but pulsating DC to power our speaker. The receiver removes everything but the changes the microphone caused in our transmitter.

Or, we could use the constantly changing frequency of sounds that our rock group is producing to modulate the carrier wave. Blend that super-fast radio frequency with the poky, slow-changing audio frequency and we have "frequency modulation," or "FM." When a receiver filters out the unmodulated carrier wave, what remains will be our immortal music.

AM radio employs subtle changes in the strength of the signal. Little power surges, like those caused by sparking motors or distant thunder, will be interpreted as part of the signal. Sparks and lightning transmit radio waves. The sound you hear as a result of them is called "static."

FM radio employs subtle changes in frequency, not strength, and is therefore affected less by little power surges. You don't hear nearly as much "static" when you listen to FM radio stations.

The Plot Thickens

I've never slept better than I did one night in late October. The cabin bunk bed was warm, and in my dream, it even smelled like it had clean sheets. As I lay under the covers in that dreamy twilight world of morning half-sleep, I thought I could hear some cartoon show on a television and the sounds of traffic outside; the sounds brought back a flood of happy Saturday-morning childhood memories.

What a pleasant dream, I thought. After months of camping far from civilization, I missed television and traffic and clean sheets, and I hadn't even realized it. I knew I'd have to rouse myself in a minute and build up the fire, but for now it was luxurious to keep my eyes closed and listen to that imaginary cartoon show.

The telephone shattered my peacefulness. I threw off the covers and reached in the direction of its terrible jangling. Fumbling through the fog of my dreaminess, I picked it up and said "hello" before I realized that the cabin didn't have a telephone.

A familiar sinister voice laughed quietly in my ear.

"Hello?" I repeated. "Who's there?" I wondered where in the world a telephone had come from. Was it one of Mike's tricks?

"Who do you think it is?" The man's voice whispered tauntingly. I had heard that voice before, somewhere, in a dream, perhaps, or a dungeon...

Suddenly I was wide awake.

"But you're, you're..."

"Imaginary?" the Magician said, then laughed quietly again. It was a Vincent Price sort of laugh. "Then you have nothing to worry about, do you?"

I looked frantically around the cabin.

Only I wasn't in the cabin any more. I was in a luxurious hotel room, with fancy wallpaper and a color television set. A cartoon show was on. I was sitting on the edge of a huge double bed.

"Where am I?" I asked nervously into the telephone.

"Boulder, Colorado," the Magician said. "And late for breakfast. Take a shower, get dressed. We'll meet you downstairs in half an hour." Then the line went dead. I hung up the phone.

"Okay, Kenn," I said to myself. "Which one is the dream?" Perhaps everything had been a dream until right now: Mike, the Magician, Belinda, all of it. Maybe that voice was just some friend I had promised to have breakfast with, and, like Dorothy in the Wizard of Oz, I had incorporated them into a fantastic dream. On the other hand, I didn't remember coming to Boulder and the note pad by the phone said "Boulder, Colorado." So maybe I'm dreaming right now, I thought.

My feet looked dirty, even for a dream, and a hot, soapy shower certainly sounded wonderful. Clean up now, sort it all out later, I decided.

I seemed to be in a big old brick hotel that had been tastefully redecorated, in the middle of downtown Boulder. Outside the window, the Rocky Mountains loomed so huge and close I could almost hear them thinking. Below on the street, cars and pedestrians played out their friendly competition without the shouts and horn-honking antics of the large cities. It sure looks like Boulder, I thought cautiously. I put on the new jeans and the University of Colorado sweatshirt I discovered in the room and went downstairs.

The restaurant off the lobby was light and open, full of plants in hanging oak planters, shiny brass rails, and stained glass shades. The young man who led me to the table was wearing jeans and a T-shirt under a tuxedo jacket. He had a ring in one ear, a great tan, and wore running shoes. Despite his relatively menial job and his outfit, he had the comfortable confidence, and the haircut, of someone who's been rich all his life.

Yes, this is Boulder, I thought, sure at last.

The Magician was already sitting at the table in his blue velvet robe, wispy gray hair partially hiding his craggy face. He's made a mistake, I thought. Even in Boulder he's going to stand out. Beside him sat Belinda, lovely as ever, studying a menu. Across the table from her I was astonished to see Mike, his green skin contrasting sharply with the new, white turtleneck sweater he wore.

"I think the vegetarian quiche looks good," the Magician said calmly as I sat down.

"Are you crazy?" I asked as soon as the young man with the earring left. The Magician looked at me with surprise in his eyes.

"Is that a poor choice?" he asked. "I've never eaten here, of course, but the waitress said that their quiche is quite good."

"Not that. I don't care what you eat!" I said. "I mean coming here, bringing us here. Perhaps you haven't noticed that my friend is green! Don't you think someone might wonder about that?"

"It's cool, bro'," Mike said. He was playing with his knife and fork, making little sparks jump between them.

"Cut that out, Mike! You don't see anybody else doing that, do you?"

"You needn't get so excited," the Magician said. "We'll only be here one day. And for this day, I think you'll find that we blend in rather well. It is, after all, a college town."

Just then a young man came up to our table. Immediately I disliked him. Perhaps it was because he was obviously interested in Belinda, or perhaps it was the fact that he was dressed like a tree. He wore rough brown coveralls with brown twigs and leaves sticking out from his back and chest. It had been a while since I'd been in Boulder, but I was sure that his outfit would not be considered stylish even here. He was a looney tune and we looked like his kind of group. He ignored the rest of us and went directly to Belinda.

"How'd you like to take a little spin in my Porsche?"

Belinda looked a little confused, but she smiled anyway.

"I'm sorry," she said softly. "I don't really care for Russian food."

The young man laughed.

"Not borscht, baby. Porsche. My car. I think you and I ought to pop over to Vail and hit the slopes. I have a condo in the village, and some lift tickets. Leave these tool heads. What do you say?"

Belinda was still confused. "Car?"

The Magician spoke quietly, without looking up.

"Belinda does not go out with trees."

"Hey, pop, butt out! I believe I was talking to the lady."

The Magician took a sip of his coffee, replaced it calmly on the table, and sat back. His face showed no emotion, but his eyes flashed from deep within their sockets. "And she would certainly never be seen with a tree that quacks like a duck."

"Hey, bud, who do you think you're talking to! I don't let anybody talk to me like that! Why, if you were just a half a century younger, I'd quack!"

The Magician looked him in the eye calmly.

"You'd what?"

"I'd quack! Quack, quack!" The young man's expression changed from arrogance to surprise, then quickly to fear as he realized that he was, indeed, quacking like a duck.

"I'm sure you'll have no problem finding another companion," the Magician said, turning his attention once again to the menu. "Someone you can communicate with." The young man stepped back from the table and pointed at the Magician threateningly.

"Quack, quack! Quack, quack!" he said angrily, then noticed that people were beginning to stare at him curiously. Quickly he turned and walked away, obviously bewildered.

"It's a small spell," the Magician said from behind the menu. "He'll be fine unless he gets near Belinda again."

Mike couldn't help it. The thought of a man dressed like a tree quacking angrily at the Magician was too silly. He started to giggle.

165

Soon Belinda and I caught his mood, and within a few seconds the three of us were laughing out loud. The Magician, not easily moved to laughter, drank his coffee. When the rest of us calmed down, he spoke again.

"I have been followed, after all," he said simply. My jaw dropped, he gestured to stop my inevitable comment. "No, it's all right. My enemies are not well-equipped to deal with magic. Nor are they any more at home in this time period than I am. I have a plan that should put an end to that problem. However, we must continue my education immediately. It would be foolish for me to stay too long in this century."

He turned to Belinda. "Perhaps you and Mike would like to go shopping for a while. Kenn and I need to discuss electronics."

I was still worried about Mike. The Magician sensed this and pointed to a group of people across the room. Each one was dressed as a werewolf. At first I thought that Boulder, always a little strange, had finally, collectively flipped out. Then I realized what day it was. The Magician nodded as he saw that I understood.

"That's right," he said. "It's Halloween."

When we finished eating, Belinda and Mike rose to leave.

"Be careful," I said.

"We shall be infinitely cool," said Mike, grinning. "I am the green onion, the man with the moves, the coolest of the cool, the grooviest of the hip cats." He started snapping his fingers in rhythm to some jazzy tune in his mind and doing bird thrusts with his head. "I am moved, daddy-o, I am moved." He and Belinda disappeared out the door, just one more incredibly beautiful medieval lady and one more green beatnik among all the werewolves, goblins, and ex-presidents wandering the downtown Boulder mall. They'll fit right in, I thought.

"I believe you were about to explain capacitors to me," the Magician said. I took a deep breath.

"If you separate two conductors with a very thin insulator, you have a capacitor." I said. "The conductors are called 'plates' and the insulator is called the 'dielectric.' For example, if you separate two sheets of aluminum foil with a piece of wax paper, you have made a capacitor. Current will flow into a capacitor because it senses the voltage across the dielectric. Once the first plate is full of Greenies..."

"Full of what?"

"I mean electrons. Once the first plate has all the electrons it can hold, the capacitor is 'charged' and no more current can flow."

"So, if you put a capacitor in a circuit, current will flow for a short period of time, and then stop?"

"Exactly. Of course, if the circuit is using alternating current, it will flow for an instant each time the current changes direction. Just until the capacitor is charged."

"Interesting."

"I think so. The faster the current alternates, the less effect a capacitor will have. If it's changing directions quickly enough, the capacitor will never have time to get fully charged, so it will never stop the current at all."

"You mean a capacitor acts like a resistor whose resistance decreases as the frequency increases?"

I stared at him.

"Boy," I said, "you're pretty good at this jargon business. That sounds like something a textbook would say."

"Well," he said modestly, "my profession does require a certain flair for words. Spells, you know, incantations, that sort of thing."

"I think you've got capacitors pretty well covered. The ability to hold a charge is measured in farads. I don't think I told you that."

"Farads," he muttered.

"If you put capacitors in series, you reduce the total capacitance," I continued. "Greenies can't hear the party music very well through more than one wall."

"What?"

"Forget I said that. What I meant to say was that you effectively increase the distance between the two plates that are directly connected to the circuit when you put capacitors in series, therefore reducing their effectiveness."

"You're going to have to do better than that."

"When you put capacitors in series, you get less total capacitance. How's that?"

"I can understand that."

"And when you put them in parallel, you increase the total surface area of the plates directly connected to the circuit, so you increase the capacitance."

"Capacitors in parallel, more capacitance."

"Exactly. To figure parallel capacitance, just add the values of all the capacitors in parallel. To figure total capacitance of capacitors in series, use this formula:"

$$C= \frac{1}{1/C1 + 1/C2 + 1/C3... \text{(etc.)}}$$

"That's a lot like resistors in parallel."

"It's the same basic formula."

"And I can use my calculator?"

"Of course."

"And my answer will be in farads?"

"Yes. Capacitance is measured in farads."

"Good. Now you may go to the bathroom."

"What?"

"It doesn't take a great magician to see that you've had four cups of coffee and you're fidgeting terribly. You're making me nervous. I'll wait here."

I felt a lot better when I came back.

"Coils," he said, as I sat down.

"What?"

"You've been thinking about coils." I just shook my head and wished he had decided to do this in Las Vegas. We could have made a fortune.

"When you coil up a wire," I said, "you get a lot of self induction. You know, opposition to any change in the amount of current that flows. The more the current tries to change, the more opposition it will encounter. It takes a while for a current to fight its way through a coil after it's first turned on. After it overcomes the self-induction and is steady, the coil acts just like a straight wire. Very little resistance."

"That sounds like the opposite of a capacitor."

168

"Well, in a lot of ways, it is."

"And a coil will constantly oppose AC."

"You are a quick study."

"I have a keen interest in learning the material."

"Right. Anyway, the higher the frequency, the more opposition it will encounter in a coil."

"And the formulas?"

"Well, inductance is measured in 'henrys'"

"Abbreviated capital 'H'?" He was making some notes on his napkin. The waiter refilled our coffee cups and I swallowed hard.

"No, actually it's abbreviated capital 'L.'"

"Is this some sort of joke?" There was an intense look about the old fellow's eyes that reminded me of our first encounter. How quickly his mood could change!

"Not at all," I said hastily. "Inductance is abbreviated with a capital L but it's measured in henrys. I told you I was new at this. It seems weird to me, too. The formulas are just the same as for resistance. If coils are in series, you add their henrys together to get the total. If they're in parallel, you use:

$$L = \frac{1}{1/L1 + 1/L2 + 1/L3 \,...(\text{etc.})}$$

There's less total inductance if they're in parallel because you've provided alternate routes."

"Hmm," he said, deep in thought. "A capacitor isn't going to be used in a circuit that just has direct current is it? I mean, what would be the point? After that first fraction of a second, it will stop all the current, like a permanent 'off' switch."

"Well, yes, I guess that's true."

"And a coil isn't going to be used in a DC circuit much either, is it? After the first instant, it might as well be just another wire. Neither one of those are used in DC circuits, are they?"

"I hadn't thought about it, but I guess you're right."

"So, in DC circuits we probably have mostly resistors, switches, and electromagnets, things like that. In an AC circuit, we'll have those things, but we're also likely to find capacitors and coils. A resistor is a resistor; AC or DC doesn't really matter. But these other two, coils and capacitors, they'll have different effects depending on the frequency of the AC."

"That's exactly right."

"I'm surprised there's not a word for it."

"Reactance," I said. "It's called 'reactance.' The opposition to current that varies with the frequency. We have capacitive reactance and inductive reactance. To figure the total opposition to current in an AC circuit, you have to take into account capacitive reactance, inductive reactance, and of course, plain old resistance. The final result is called 'impedance.'"

"And you just add them all up?"

"No, you can't do that. Capacitive reactance and inductive reactance tend to cancel each other out. You figure out one, then the other, and subtract the smaller one from the bigger one. If a circuit has 70 ohms of capacitive reactance and 100 ohms of inductive reactance, there will be only 30 ohms of reactance detectable, and it will be inductive reactance. Using a special formula, you add that to the resistance, and you'll know how much impedance a circuit has."

Since that was all I knew about reactance and impedance, I quickly moved on.

"Then we come to transformers."

"Go ahead."

"A transformer is two coils of wire so close to each other that the lines of magnetism from one cross the other one, inducing a current in it."

"That sounds simple enough."

"Well, it is. The first coil is called the primary. That's the one hooked up to your source of voltage. The other coil is called the secondary. It isn't plugged into anything, because it gets its power by inductance, from the primary."

"Why would you want one of those?"

I thought for a minute. "Sometimes you don't want two parts of a circuit to be directly connected. Magnetic coupling, using a transformer, can do that. Also, if the secondary has more turns of wire than the primary, it will have more voltage. If it has less turns than the primary, it will have less voltage".

"That sounds like magic."

"Not really. The price you pay for increasing the voltage is that you have less current. On the other hand, if you step down the voltage, you'll have more current. It's more like business than magic."

"So, you can use a transformer to change the voltage of alternating current."

"Right. If you want to increase the voltage, you use a step-up transformer. If you want to decrease the voltage, you use a step-down transformer. Most transformers are wound around some sort of iron core. The whole thing tends to get hot because of little eddy currents..."

"Little Eddie who?"

"Little eddy currents. You know, stray currents induced in the iron. They make a transformer less efficient. Besides overcoming self-induction, a transformer has to overcome the resistance in all that wire wound around the core, and it has to overcome hysteresis, the iron's opposition to a change in magnetic polarity."

"Transformers tend to get hot," the Magician said. "Fine. How about radio?"

"Radio is like a transformer without the iron core," I said. "The transmitter is the primary, the receiver is the secondary. The transmitter induces a current in the receiver. If the current is alternating very fast in the primary..."

"You mean if it is high-frequency AC?"

"Yes. High-frequency current produces a magnetic field that also alternates very fast. This high-frequency field extends for a great distance from the transmitter. We call it electromagnetic waves. If it falls within a certain range of frequencies we call it radio waves, or a radio signal. Other frequencies are called microwaves, or radar or television waves. They can travel for thousands of miles, if there is enough current in the transmitter. Actually, we pick up radio signals from stars that are millions of miles away."

"Radio signals from the stars? I had no idea."

"There is no message, of course. It's just naturally occurring bursts of radio frequency energy."

"You don't believe anyone is transmitting a message?"

"Of course not."

"Yet you believe in magic."

"No, I don't. That would be silly."

"Then how are you doing that?"

"Doing what?"

He didn't say anything, but reached for his coffee cup. I was puzzled and nervous, but couldn't tell that I was doing anything very remarkable.

"You must teach me that science sometime," he said, putting his cup back down. With a start I realized that the chair I sat in was floating about a foot off the ground. Before I could react, it began to spin slowly, with me in it. No one seemed to be looking, and I resisted the temptation to scream. I found myself facing away from the table. The chair continued to rotate until I was back in my original position. Then it settled gently back to the floor.

"I believe you were explaining how you believed in neither magic nor messages from space."

"I think we better stick to electronics."

"Ah, yes, electronics. And specifically, radio."

"Right. We have these high-frequency radio waves being caused by a transmitter. Miles away they are inducing a very fast alternating current in some wire. The wire is hooked up to a speaker. Only the current is alternating so fast that the electromagnet in the speaker can't keep up. Self-induction and hysteresis make it sluggish. So we add a diode to the circuit."

"I don't know that word."

"A diode is a component that has two parts. Current will pass through a diode easily in one direction, but will be stopped in the reverse direction."

"A one-way valve."

"Exactly. The diode allows pulses of current to reach the electromagnet in the speaker. Since they're all headed the same direction, the magnet doesn't have to reverse polarities."

172

"Excuse me?"

"The north pole of the magnet doesn't have to become a south pole. It's always a north. It's just a little stronger every time a pulse goes through its coil. Since sound waves are so much slower than radio waves, you might have a thousand of these pulses for each little pull on the speaker. A diode that's used like this is called a detector."

"Because it allows the receiver to detect radio signals?"

"I guess so. Radio has become more complicated than this. We've added circuits to make the sound clearer, to tune in specific stations, and to make the sound louder. But basically it still works the same."

"Excellent. Now, I'm afraid we have to stop our little lesson."

"But I haven't covered vacuum tube diodes..."

"We can finish later tonight. My enemies have found me."

"You mean..."

"Precisely. A scientist from the future has overcome his fear of time travel, overcome the Committee Spell, and has arrived in Boulder. I shall have to set my plan in motion immediately. I suggest you return to your room and write. This evening, if all goes well, we may continue. Afterward, perhaps we can find a celebration to attend."

"You mean a party?"

"Will you never run out of jargon?"

I smiled and motioned for the waitress to bring the check. An instant later, when I looked back, the Magician had vanished.

"Yes, I'll be happy to take care of that for you," the waitress said, handing the breakfast bill to me. I knew she meant she'd carry my money over to the cash register for me. Only I knew that my wallet was empty.

"If he thinks that's some great magic trick, disappearing when the bill comes, he really is from the Dark Ages!" I muttered. "Just about all my friends do that one."

"Excuse me?" The waitress was still smiling.

"Nothing. Listen, we're all staying at the hotel. Would you charge this to our rooms?"

"Of course. Just sign here."

I put my room number on the bill, added a big tip to the total, and signed my name. If he could figure how to get us into the hotel, he could figure out how to pay for it, I thought.

Then I went up to my room and began to write as fast as I could.

Superconductors

Everything has at least some resistance. Whenever electricity travels through any substance, part of its energy is converted to heat because of this resistance, and therefore is wasted. There is one remarkable and mysterious exception.

Early in the 20th century it was discovered that if you cool mercury nearly to absolute zero (about 450 degrees below regular zero), suddenly it loses all its resistance. All of it. It becomes a "superconductor." If you send a pulse of electricity through a closed loop of a superconducting material, it will keep going 'round and 'round forever.

This was a harmless novelty for years. It is expensive to cool things to absolute zero in the first place, and no one had a good explanation why it happened in the second place. Whenever these two conditions exist (expensive, hard to explain) phenomena are shuffled into the footnotes of textbooks and declared to be unimportant.

In the 1980s, scientists discovered that some specially prepared mixtures of metallic oxides become superconductors at much warmer temperatures. Of course, the electron theory guys whined. This wasn't supposed to happen. The theory didn't predict it. Once they realized the implications of the discovery, they shut up and started working. In the daytime they taught undergraduates the electron theory. At night, in their basements, unburdened by their formal beliefs, they mixed different combinations of stuff like alchemists, hoping to get lucky. The intense gleam in their eyes is not hard to understand.

Vast quantities of energy (pronounced "money") are wasted every hour by producing electricity that is lost when it is turned, by resistance, into heat. Millions of dollars per hour. If you could figure out how to produce cheap superconductors that would work at a fairly warm temperature, you could save the world a huge amount of wasted energy.

You could probably even earn a little of that energy yourself.

Semi-Conductors and Junction Diodes

Remember your cat-zapping days? Your love of static electricity? Of course you do. Every normal person goes through a pith-ball phase; it's nothing to be ashamed of. Those rare individuals who never develop the urge to rub some amber against a sheep are the guys we have to worry about.

At any rate, you probably recall that some materials tend to develop a positive charge and other materials are more inclined to develop a negative charge. Black combs pick up scraps of paper because of their negative charge, glass rods because of their positive charge. This characteristic is simply built into the nature of the material. "P-type" materials develop a positive charge, while "N-type" materials develop a negative charge. Materials that naturally tend to develop either kind of static charge are usually rotten conductors of electricity, and most of the electrical activity takes place on their surfaces. As you also recall, electricity moves from a negative charge toward a positive charge. The spark leaps from the cat nose to the window, but not the reverse.

To take advantage of this, you could make a diode by mounting a cat against a glass window, but that program may not please the cat. Electricity would flow more easily in the "cat-to-window" direction than it would in the "window-to-cat" direction. You will find that this device works best if you leave a tiny gap between the two elements, so that both the window and the cat can develop good charges at their closest points.

The "window-cat diode" is a solid-state device; that is, it does not employ a vacuum. It has some disadvantages as an electrical component, however. Both the cat and the window have too much resistance, for one thing. Unless a circuit provides a lot of voltage, no current will flow, but that much voltage may cause your component to squirm and yowl. Luckily, scientists have discovered other "P-type" and "N-type" materials that do not need to be fed and let out at night. Impure crystals of silicon can be either type, depending on their impurities. Along with other materials, impure silicon crystals are called semiconductors, because they rate somewhere between good conductors and good insulators.

The area where "P-type" material touches "N-type" material is called the "P-N Junction." Most of the electrical activity occurs at that junction. In the manufacturing process, a very thin "no-man's land" is produced at the junction called the "depletion zone." The depletion zone is where the P- and N- type materials have melted together. It is of neither type, and provides a little barrier to the Greenies a few molecules thick. It separates the cat from the window.

Girl Greenies tend to gather near the junction in the "P" section, because it seems like a good place to have a party. They open a couple of kegs of beer, turn on their little radios, and wait. Boy Greenies in the "N" section will tend to build up along the junction, on their side of the depletion zone, because they're attracted to the positive charge.

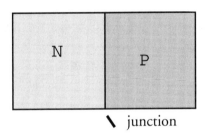

\ junction

A "P-N Junction Diode" will act just like a vacuum tube diode or a cat's whisker diode in a circuit. Electricity will only go through it in one direction. Greenie guys are poised to leap across the junction from the N side to the P side. They need only a little push. It will, however, take a bulldozer to make them leave the party just so they can go stand in line again. This tension along the junction is important. Just as a cat does not have a "charge" unless you pet it, and clouds don't have a charge unless the wind stirs up the water droplets, so a junction diode does not have this tension across the depletion zone when it's sitting in the store window. You have to add a little energy. You add this energy by sending a tiny bit of electricity through the diode, or heating it, or letting light shine upon it. Most kinds of diodes require just a quick snort of electricity to become charged, and it happens so fast you'll never notice.

A junction diode can fit on the head of a pin. When you buy one at the store, it will be enclosed in a little gob of hard plastic, with wires already attached so you can use it without a microscope. It works just like a big old vacuum tube diode: Current can only get through in one direction. Since it has no vacuum, it is a solid-state device. It is also a semiconductor. Unlike the vacuum tube, it does not require a hot filament, which uses a lot of power. It does not have a fragile glass enclosure, dangerous because of its vacuum. It is tough and efficient.

In the middle of the 20th century, scientists began figuring out cheap ways to make solid state devices that use P-N junctions. This development changed the world, much as the discovery of sheep had changed the world centuries earlier. It made possible computers, video games, space travel and some really neat rock 'n' roll effects.

Junction Diode:
A Crisis on Elm Street

"Throw down your weapons and come out peacefully!" The policeman's voice was distorted by the bullhorn. "We've got you surrounded!" The young officer waited a moment, then turned to his partner. "It's no use. They're ignoring us."

Just then, the chief of police pulled up. He was a big man, over two-hundred pounds, with curly black hair and a deep voice. He was a tough, no-nonsense fellow, strong and athletic. You didn't mess with "the Chief," as everyone called him. He had been called away from a fancy dinner party at the mayor's mansion, for which he was grateful, and still wore the tuxedo. No one commented on it. As he walked over to the little group of policemen, his mind cataloged information. An ordinary block, he thought. Little houses, all pretty much the same, nice lawns. This was probably the most excitement they'd had around here for a while. The SWAT team was just arriving, policemen were roping off the area. His men had already evacuated the civilians.

"What's the story?" he asked, when he reached the young man with the bullhorn. "I just got the call."

The officer filled him in quickly. "We've got the house surrounded, sir. Marksmen on the roof across the street, plainclothesmen in the alley. Telescope surveillance front and rear. There's no way they can get out of there without us knowing about it."

"Good work. Give me that thing." the Chief took the bullhorn. "Throw down your weapons and come out of there! We've got you surrounded!" He waited but nothing happened. "They're ignoring us, aren't they?"

"Yes sir."

Suddenly another question occurred to the Chief.

"Who's in there, anyway?"

"It's the darndest thing, sir. It's chickens."

"What?"

"That's right, sir. Chickens. Hundreds of them. They must have escaped from the pound or something. They've taken over this house."

"From the pound? The dog pound?"

The young officer's partner took over.

"He's a city boy, Chief. That's where he thinks animals come from. Now, I think these are circus chickens."

The Chief ignored their opinions for the moment.

"Are there hostages?"

"No sir. Just the chickens. And they've made no demands. We don't know if they're armed or not, but I say we take no chances. That SWAT team should be in position pretty soon..."

"Hmm." The Chief was deep in thought. "That's a new one. Chickens."

"Yes sir. Here's the layout." One of the officers unrolled a blueprint of the house. "Here's the front door. The only other way out is the back door. We've got that covered from the alley."

"What's this area here?" The Chief began to take charge of the situation by organizing the information at hand.

178

"The entire front section of the house has a tile floor. The back section has carpeting."

"What kind of carpeting?"

"It's a lovely white plush carpet, sir. I'd love to have some like that in my family room…"

The Chief marked on the blueprint. "Okay, we're going to call this back section of the house 'P' for 'plush carpet.'"

"Whatever you say, sir."

"And the front section here has no carpeting?"

"That's right."

"Then we'll call this front section 'N' for 'no carpet.' Got that? Now we're getting somewhere. Where's that telescope surveillance information?"

"Here I am, sir." A young woman officer stepped forward. "Officer Dickinson."

"What's going on in there, Dickinson?"

"Break-dancing, sir."

"What?"

"Break-dancing. It's a kind of dancing where you slide around a lot and do fancy athletic maneuvers. The chickens are break-dancing."

"Why would they do that?"

The young woman shrugged.

"Why would anybody?" she answered. "They're probably from the circus. As far as I can tell, they're not threatening anyone else. They're just dancing. It looks like nearly all of them are in the front section of the house."

"The 'N' section?"

"Excuse me?"

"The section with no carpeting?"

"Of course. You can't break-dance on carpet, sir. There's a few in the back, walking around. That's all I can tell so far."

"Good work, Dickinson."

"Excuse me, excuse me." A small man with very thick glasses was trying to get through the crowd of policemen.

"Get him out of here!" the Chief bellowed, waving his hand. The young woman officer, Dickinson, leaned over to the Chief.

"He's from the governor's office," she whispered. "His name is Smedley." The Chief nodded.

"Is that Mr. Smedley? Let that man through! For heaven's sake, men, use some common sense." He reached out to shake the man's hand. "Good to see you, Smedley, appreciate your coming down. Everyone calls me Chief."

"Pleased to meet you, Chief, I'm from the governor's Crisis Control office."

"Let me fill you in..." the Chief stopped as Smedley held up his hand and smiled grimly. He was thin and pale and looked worried. The Chief couldn't imagine Smedley being much help. It seemed like whenever there was a crisis, the governor sent someone who looked like Woody Allen.

"It's pretty obvious what you've got here," Smedley said. "It's another chicken take-over, isn't it?"

"Another? You mean..." The Chief's mouth fell open in astonishment.

"We've been trying to keep a lid on it. What do you figure, five-hundred, a thousand of them? Was anyone home when they did it?"

"No, the owners are out of town."

"That's good. It can get dangerous in there once they start break-dancing."

The Chief just nodded.

"You've tried the bullhorn?"

"They just ignore us."

Smedley laughed, perhaps louder than was necessary.

"They're not ignoring you, Chief. They can't hear you. You get a thousand crazed chickens break-dancing in a house and it gets pretty noisy. No, we're going to have to do better than the bullhorn. You're lucky I'm here."

"What are you going to do?"

"There's one sound that just might break through their concentration."

"What's that?"

"The sound of a metal scoop plunging into a bucket of grain. That sound means dinner time to chickens all over the world. It's our only chance."

"Are you sure you're from the governor's office?"

"Yes sir. We have this problem all the time."

"Well, let's give it a try then. What do we do?"

"We'll park a big truck in front of the house and put a ramp out its back doors. I'll take a bucket of grain into the truck and scoop some of it out. Then stand back!"

"But how will they hear that?"

"We only need one chicken to hear it, sir. If a chicken hears that sound, he gets excited and lets out a loud screech. Sort of a dinner time war cry. The rest will follow him."

It didn't seem like a good plan, but it was better than no plan. And Smedley was, after all, from the governor's office. The policemen sprang into action. A truck was parked in front of the house, a bucket of grain was obtained, and a metal scoop. Smedley walked up the ramp. He insisted on doing it himself. The crowd held its breath as he began scooping grain. Two scoops... three... four...

Nothing happened.

Finally Smedley came out of the truck, little beads of sweat glistening on his forehead. His voice was tense.

"I don't understand," he said. "Do you have a diagram of the house?" The blueprint was unrolled once more. "What's this area labeled 'P'?" he asked.

"Plush carpet," the Chief answered. "I guess it's a lovely white..."

"Not any more," Smedley said. "And this section near the front of the house labeled 'N'?"

"No carpet."

"That's it, then!" Smedley said, obviously relieved. "They're all break-dancing at the front of the house. We'll never get their attention. Is there an alley behind the house?"

"Yes, there is!"

"Good, move this truck back there. There will be a few chickens walking around on that plush carpet, the 'P' section, as you call it. They'll hear the scoop. Now we've got them!"

181

The truck was moved, the ramp was lowered, the crowd held its breath. Smedley plunged the metal scoop into the bucket of grain.

Almost instantly there was a blood-curdling screech from the house and a chicken raced out the back door. It stopped and looked around, feathers askew, a wild expression on his face. Smedley plunged the scoop into the bucket a second time. The chicken screeched again and began running toward the truck. This time there were dozens of other screeches, and chickens began pouring out the back door. Smedley leaped out of the truck just in time to avoid being crushed by the stampede. When the last chicken had raced up the ramp, the policemen removed it and closed the truck doors, capturing every chicken without firing a shot.

"Take 'em downtown and cook 'em!" the Chief roared. "I mean book 'em!" The truck pulled away, and the press closed in on Smedley.

"This was an isolated incident," he said, "and the governor would appreciate your helping us keep publicity to a minimum. There is no need to panic the public, and besides, we'd hate to trigger any copy-cat chicken incidents."

"Mr. Smedley, why did the chickens respond when you were behind the house, but not in front of the house?"

"That's elementary poultry psychology," he replied. "The key is to understand the P-N Junction, the place where the tile floor meets the carpet. The 'N' section, having no carpeting will be full of chickens, all break dancing. The 'P' section, having plush carpeting, is relatively useless for dancing, and will have few chickens. Now, it's easy for a chicken to leave the dance floor and step onto the carpet, if one ever wanted to. There's lots of room. But it's tough to step off the carpet onto the tile. It's already full of dancing chickens, and you're likely to get a wing in the neck. Luckily, chickens would rather eat than dance. So, in a chicken caper involving a 'P-N Junction' you've got to lure your chickens out the 'P' side of the house. You'll never get them out the 'N' side. Once the dance floor is full, the junction between tile and carpet is like a one-way chicken valve."

Another reporter stuck a microphone in Smedley's face.

"Isn't that similar to the way a P-N junction diode works in electricity?"

Smedley got very red in the face.

"No comment," he said.

"Don't duck the issue, Mr. Smedley! We're live right now on Channel 4, and I think our viewers would like to hear your answer. Doesn't electricity only travel one direction across a PN Junction? Doesn't it always go from the 'N' side to the 'P' side? And isn't that just like what happened here today? I think our viewers would like to know the governor's position on the relationship between chickens and electricity. Don't you agree, Mr. Smedley?"

"No comment."

Transistors

Electricity moves across a P-N Junction in the "N" to "P" direction fairly easily. It does not move in the opposite direction easily at all. This is why a P-N Junction diode works.

A transistor is a sandwich made of "P" material and "N" material. When the "bread" is made of "P" type material, and the salami is "N" type material, it is called a PNP transistor:

At first glance, a transistor would appear to be the result of a government study to improve the diode: It stops current in both directions. No matter which way electricity tries to go, it has to go through one junction the "wrong" way, from P to N. Since it can't do that, it stops:

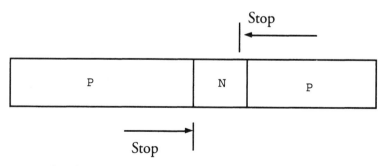

Consider the NPN transistor for a moment. If we want current to flow, we must eliminate the negative charges at the junctions. Since the Greenies already want to leap into the P section, the easiest solution is to attach a wire to the P section, hire a little bitty rock 'n roll band, and lead them to the party. That is to say, connect the P section to the positive side of a battery and connect either one of the N sections to the negative side of the battery, and drain away the charge:

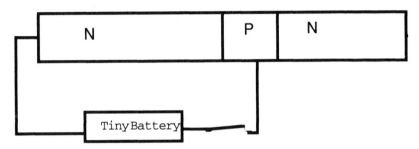

Greenies from both N sections will leap across their junction into the P section, into the wire, and toward the battery. Now the transistor has no charges at all along its junctions, and current will flow through it easily. The junctions will still tend to develop charges, but it will take a little time. As long as our control circuit is set up, it will keep draining the charges away as fast as they can form. If we disconnect our control circuit, the charges will reestablish themselves. In this circuit:

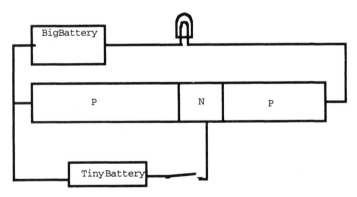

we have two circuits using the same transistor. Our little bitty control circuit is powered by a tiny little hearing aid battery like the kind that powers electric watches. That circuit contain a switch.

Our big, powerful circuit is powered by a massive truck battery and contains a truck headlight. The headlight is off because electricity can't get through the transistor. The charge at the PN junction stops it.

We close the switch in our little bitty control circuit. The hearing-aid battery lures the junction Greenies into the P section, then out of the transistor altogether.

Suddenly the headlight comes on! Without the obstruction of the charged junctions in the transistor, current from the truck battery can flow through the transistor, completing the circuit. If we open the switch in our little control circuit, the charges quickly reestablish themselves, and the headlight goes out again.

When you read that again you will see that we can use a tiny circuit, without much voltage or current, to control a much larger current and voltage.

That is exactly what we use transistors for.

A transistor can be either a NPN sandwich or a PNP sandwich. That could create some confusion, so we name the three sections. The middle section is called the "base," and the other two are the "collector" and "emitter." In a PNP transistor, the base is made of "N" type material, while both the collector and emitter are made of "P" type material. An NPN transistor is just the opposite. They work the same, except that you have to connect the negative side of the battery to the base in a NPN transistor to turn on your headlight. Sometimes that's handier.

The original transistor was a cat's whisker diode, with two cat's whiskers. One was the emitter, the other the collector. The large, flat connection on the opposite side of the crystal was the base. It was invented by three Norwegian scientists working for Bell Laboratories in 1949. I'm sure many people thought they were foolish. After all, the cat's whisker diode had become a quaint historical footnote by that time, an electrical dinosaur, all but extinct. Thanks to the electron theory and a successful campaign of electrical jargon, the world had been largely saved from spark-gap transmitters and crystal sets. They didn't seem so fun anymore. Had the science teachers been able to come up with just a few more complicated words and formulas, they might have been able to save the world from the invention of the transistor.

The Triode

Remember Thomas Alva's vacuum tube diode? It was a jar containing two elements: a hot filament (or cathode) and a plate of metal. The two elements were separated by a vacuum. Current would flow from the filament to the plate, but not "backward."

A triode is just a diode with a metal screen or grid between the cathode and the plate. By itself, the screen has no effect on the circuit. Greenies stream right through it.

However, a slight negative charge on this grid will stop the current. By placing the grid close to the cathode, a tiny change in its charge will have a huge effect on the current, just as a small twist of a water valve will have a dramatic effect on the amount of water shooting out your garden hose. For that reason, triodes were once called "valves" and still are in Great Britain. Before the invention of the transistor, triodes were used in thousands of circuits which required that a small voltage or current control a much larger one.

Picture, if you will, a million turkeys milling around in a desert valley surrounded by hills. These are hungry turkeys, but they're dumb. They don't realize that they are being used in some bizarre analogy in which they represent Greenies massed around the filament of a triode. All they know is that it's been a couple of days since they've eaten, they're surrounded by hills, and they don't know which direction to move.

There is a pickup truck on top of one of the hills, and a man standing beside it. The turkeys are curious, but suspicious. There could be grain in that truck; on the other hand, the man could be a turkey butcher. They wait. The truck represents the grid in a triode, without any charge. The turkeys have some voltage, but no place to go. The stage is set.

Suddenly the man reaches into the bed of the truck, picks up a handful of cracked corn and throws it down the hill toward the turkeys.

If you have never heard a million turkeys shriek their corn-attack gobble in unison, it may be hard for you to imagine the sound those birds make as they race up the hill. They move together, a huge feathered amoebae flowing toward the truck, thundering like an army of amateur yodelers.

When they reach the top of the hill, the pickup truck is quickly forgotten as they see what lies beyond: The entire valley is filled with cracked corn as far as the eye can see. Enough corn to swim in. The corn, of course, is the plate of the triode, with its positive charge. Very few turkeys stop at the truck. Like a gobbling, waddling river they flow over the hill and immerse themselves in all that wonderful grain.

Until the man in the pickup truck picks up his shotgun. The turkeys that are beyond him don't notice. They're running downhill toward the corn. But the turkeys racing up the hill toward the truck stop dead in their tracks. They're dumb, but even they know about Thanksgiving. Anyway, since they haven't reached the top of the hill, they don't know what's on the other side. The shotgun, of course, is a negative charge on the grid. It stops the current.

A smaller negative charge (perhaps the man in the truck is only wielding a pocket knife, not a shotgun) will reduce the flow of turkeys, but not stop it altogether. Some turkeys will take their chances in hand-to-claw combat.

This is another example of an everyday situation that is a lot like electronics. A single man in a truck with a bucket of corn and a weapon can control the movement of millions of turkeys. In the same way, a tiny charge on the grid of a triode can control a large current of electricity.

Historical Note

Electronic devices can be divided into two categories: solid-state devices (like junction diodes, cat's whisker diodes, and transistors) and vacuum tube devices (like vacuum tube diodes and triodes). They keep taking turns at being old-fashioned. Parlor tricks were done with solid-state toys: cats, windows, sheep, and pith balls.

Then Edison invented the vacuum tube diode, but considered it a mere oddity, a historical curiosity without much practical application. Science moved on.

A solid-state device, the cat's whisker diode, led the world into the age of electronics. A whole generation studied them, became fascinated by electronics because of them, and built devices that employed them.

Once vacuum tubes became cheap and practical, however, cat's whisker diodes and crystal sets were considered hopelessly primitive and old-fashioned. Nobody studied them much. The next generation of electronics experts learned vacuum tube technology. They built our radios, televisions, and early computers with vacuum tubes. Solid-state devices like the old cat's whisker were only discussed nostalgically, by older fellows who remembered the "good old days" of radio. They were given brief treatment in the text books as historical curiosities.

That all changed when the transistor was invented. This close relative of the cat's whisker diode could do everything a triode could do, but it didn't require a hot filament, which wastes energy. It could be manufactured cheaply, in tiny sizes; it was sturdy and reliable, and lasted longer in service than any tube. Within 25 years, the transistor had virtually replaced the vacuum tube. By 1980 you couldn't give away a television set made with vacuum tubes. By 1990, except for some specialized uses, tubes were non-existent, totally replaced by solid-state devices. Tubes were mentioned only briefly in the textbooks, as historical curiosities, and discussed nostalgically by older fellows who remembered the "good old days" of radio, when everyone used tubes.

Do you notice a pattern developing here? History loves to repeat itself. Had you and I been around in the mid-1940s, would we have been willing to look silly by fooling around with the hopelessly old-fashioned solid-state technology that had gone out of favor a generation earlier? Can you imagine what our friends and teachers would have said? They would have thought us crazy and rejected our science fair projects. Yet that's what the guys at Bell Laboratories did. They played with cat's whisker diodes.

With the money Bell Laboratories could have made on the patent for the transistor, it might have purchased several small countries. The government decided it was too good an invention for one company to monopolize, so they made them license it cheaply to anyone who wanted to use it. In retrospect, the transistor seems like a pretty good idea. Solid-state electronics has revolutionized every phase of our lives.

With that in mind, I wonder if the old vacuum tube will also spring back into use in the future with some new twist. I wonder, if you're deep in space, for example, surrounded by a vacuum, could you use vacuum tubes without the glass enclosures? Will we build fantastic computers in space using principles forgotten since the days of "black-and-white" TV? Will some neat property of vacuum tubes revolutionize life in a future century the way solid state electronics revolutionized the last half of the 20th?

Will you be the person that figures it out and gets the patent?

The Amplifier

The word "amplifier" causes a lot of confusion. To "amplify" means "to make something become larger." We all want to amplify our bank accounts, for example. So, when we hear about an electrical device called an "amplifier," we think it somehow, perhaps magically, makes something bigger.

But that's not exactly right. Electrical amplifiers don't really increase anything. They are devices in which a small current or voltage controls a larger voltage or current.

The man with the shotgun is not manufacturing turkeys; he is not making the flock larger. He is just controlling it. Very slight changes in his mood affect the huge flow of turkeys over the hill dramatically. In the same way, by using an amplifier, small changes in a little circuit can cause major changes in a much larger circuit. Amplifiers use either triodes or transistors.

Let's go back to our crystal set. If we use a battery to power the speaker, and use the faint incoming radio signal to control the battery circuit, it will seem like we made the faint signal stronger, and the sound louder. We will say that we amplified the signal. That means we used it to control a much larger current.

our fancy transistor light switch:

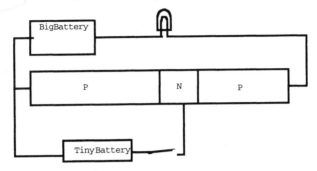

Once again we have a large battery and light in one circuit. We will call this the power circuit, and it is connected to the emitter and collector of the transistor. We also have a small control circuit that contains a small battery and a switch, connected to the emitter and base.

So far, our transistor is merely a fancy switch for the power circuit. The transistor controls whether the main circuit is on or off.

Now we add a microphone to the control circuit. This particular microphone is really a variable resistor whose resistance changes as sound waves strike it. Many microphones work like that.

When no sound is striking the microphone, it has lots of resistance, and Greenies will be unable to escape the PN junctions. The charges in the transistor will prevent electricity from flowing through it. The light will stay off.

If we hum softly into the microphone, it will have less resistance, some of the charges will be removed from the junctions, some current will be able to flow, and the light will glow dimly.

If we shout into the mike, its resistance will go way down, all the charges will leave the junctions, and the light will flash brightly.

Each change in our voice will have a dramatic effect on the light.

We replace the light with headphones or a speaker. Now our power circuit will produce sound, rather than light. Each subtle change in our voice causes a similar change in the resistance of the microphone, which changes how much current can get through the power circuit. These changes affect the sound that the speaker is making. If you're lucky, the speaker will repeat the sounds that you have made into the microphone exactly. If there is a lot of current flowing through the power circuit, the sound it produces will be much louder than the sound of your voice.

You have amplified your voice.

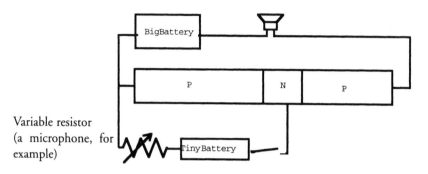

Variable resistor (a microphone, for example)

Bias Voltage

If you build the little amplifier we just discussed and turn it on, do not be surprised if nothing happens. You'll get used to turning on your little projects only to have nothing happen. Edison, optimist that he was, described it best after fooling around unsuccessfully with a project for a long time: "I now know 10,000 things that won't work as storage batteries." Of course, he didn't have the advantage of a book like this to guide him.

The many variables in the simplest circuit represent many opportunities for little mistakes. In our amplifier, for example, we used a transistor. But what transistor did we use? They come in many sizes and shapes, with different characteristics. Did we select the right battery for the control circuit? Of course, that depends on the resistance of our microphone. How much voltage does our speaker require, and how much current? How much resistance does it have? What size is the battery in the power circuit?

Each factor is dependent on all the other factors. For this reason, it is often smart to let some other poor fellow fool around with various-sized components, drive himself and his family crazy, and then simply buy the schematic he finally produces. Libraries, book stores, and electronics stores are full of books with neat plans, with the values of all the components worked out for you. By now you know much more about electronics than you need to build these projects with confidence. When somebody says they built their own stereo, that does not mean they designed it. They probably paid 10 dollars for a schematic and soldered the parts together.

One reason that your amplifier might not work is because your control battery was the wrong voltage. Since it takes less than one volt to clear the charges out of a typical transistor, and you can't buy a battery that small at the grocery store, your transistor probably never did develop any charges along the junctions. It acted like a straight wire in your circuit. Unless, of course, your microphone had a lot of resistance. In that case, you may actually need more voltage in your control circuit, just to overcome the microphone's resistance. The trick is to maintain the right amount of voltage in the control circuit, usually by adding resistors or taking them away. Voltage in the control circuit is called "bias voltage," and it determines just how much resistance the transistor will have.

Most circuits don't use two batteries. They use one power source to provide both the bias voltage and the voltage for the main circuit. They split up the circuit into two parts. This makes it tougher to decipher the schematics, but does not affect the principle. Every amplifier has a power circuit and a control circuit. The bias voltage is what appears in the control circuit.

Amplifying Chickens: Break-Dance Basketball

The Chief pulled into the high school parking lot.

"Darn!" he thought, as he saw several news vans and dozens of reporters milling around. "We'll never keep this one off the news!"

He was right, of course. A state championship basketball game had been stopped with a full half remaining and the score tied. Stopped, as I'm sure you've guessed, by chickens. The media would not be able to resist.

The Chief slipped inside through a side door and went directly to the gym. His men met him but they didn't have to say anything. The scene was self-explanatory.

Hundreds and hundreds of chickens filled the basketball court, all dancing wildly on the wooden floor. Its smooth surface was ideal for their sliding and spinning gyrations. Down the center of the court was a strip of red carpet, five or six feet wide, that had been unrolled during halftime as part of an awards ceremony. Very few chickens were on the carpet, of course, but they were bunched up tightly on each side of it.

The stands were full of angry parents and students, all red-faced and outraged, yelling obscenities at the sea of fowl, but to no avail. The two basketball teams stared glumly at each other from their benches on opposite ends of the strip of red carpet. It looked like the game would have to be cancelled.

"Is it just me," the Chief said, to no one in particular as he surveyed the scene, "or does it seem like this generation of chickens has lost all respect for tradition? Why, I remember when a chicken's place was at Sunday dinner, near the gravy..."

"Chief!"

The Chief turned toward the familiar voice.

"Smedley! Boy am I glad to see you!" There was relief in his voice. Smedley had become the Clint Eastwood of chicken crises.

"Thanks, Chief, but this is a new one for me, too. They've never taken over a basketball game before. I'm not sure what to do. I've sent for a truck, but it will be a while before it can get here."

"We can't wait for the truck," the Chief said. "This crowd is about ready to take the law into its own hands. We're not equipped to handle a full-scale chicken riot. No, we've got to get this basketball game started again somehow, as quickly as we can. Even with the chickens."

"Sir?"

"Yes?" The Chief turned to the young woman officer. "It's Dickinson, isn't it?" She had a paper in her hand.

"Yes sir. Here's the way it looks out there. The chickens are spread out fairly evenly under each of the hoops. There are very few on the

193

carpet. However, they're bunched up pretty tight on each side of the carpet."

"Why is that?"

She shrugged.

"I guess it's just to make the analogy a little better. Anyway, I've labeled the areas on the map the way you did last time. The little checks stand for chicks. You, know, chickens."

This is the diagram she gave to the Chief:

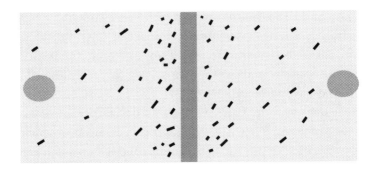

"Hmm," Smedley muttered, looking over the Chief's shoulders. "That gives me an idea. If all those chickens weren't concentrated around the carpet, you could probably play a little basketball."

"It would be messy."

"Look at that crowd, Dickinson!" Smedley spoke passionately. "Can't you see the hate in their eyes? Can't you feel that mass hysteria building? We don't have time to worry about 'messy'! We have to get some kind of basketball game started, even if there are a few chickens underfoot."

Dickinson and the Chief looked at the crowd, listened to their hoarse screaming, and knew that once again Smedley was right.

"What do we do?" the Chief asked.

"You tell the coaches to get their boys out among the chickens. I'll take care of that dense concentration along the carpet. Let's play basketball!"

Within moments the two teams of players were walking gingerly among the dancing fowl. They did not look happy. They could dribble a little, if they were careful, and even jog around. There was no way they would be able to break through that flock near the carpet, though. The crowd settled down a bit, as the players began to toss a basketball around. A few could even detect a certain humor in the situation. Everyone waited to see what would happen. If only Smedley could convince all those chickens clustered at center court to step onto the strip of red carpet, and then walk along it to the sidelines, the evening's performance would be saved.

Suddenly a group of cheerleaders ran out onto the carpet. They were holding signs that said, "Free Lemonade, This Way" with an arrow pointing to the sidelines. Sure enough, the chickens, hot and thirsty from all their dancing, leaped onto the strip of carpet and followed the cheerleaders off the court. Once on the sidelines, they kept in an orderly line, filing past the soft drink table. Smedley himself gave each one a paper cup full of ice-cold lemonade. Each chicken drained his cup in a single gulp, threw it into the trash, and followed the chicken ahead of him. Smedley didn't want to risk any of the chickens escaping before the truck arrived, so he led the line back to a corner of the court, where they rejoined the party.

The basketball game began immediately, but it was not a fast paced game. The dancing chickens created resistance to running. However, without the dense concentration of chickens around the carpet, both teams could move back and forth across the court, and after a while, most players ignored them.

An observant fan might have noticed an interesting pattern to the game. Each time a certain cheerleader walked past Smedley's table, he became a bit distracted and befuddled. His coordination level plummeted, and he distributed lemonade less efficiently. When that happened, the line of chickens backed up. Once again the basketball players were faced with a dense poultry concentration at center court, and the game slowed considerably. When the cheerleader moved on, Smedley quickly regained his composure, the lemonade was speedily dispensed, and the tempo of the basketball game increased. Had either of the coaches been observant, they could have influenced the game's outcome by directing the random meanderings of this one cheerleader, sending her to get lemonade only when the opposing team had the ball, for example. Neither coach noticed the pattern.

The basketball game ended before the truck arrived, and Smedley was able to close his lemonade stand without incident. The stands emptied, leaving the gymnasium to the clucking revelers, who continued to dance to a music heard by very few outside their species. The policemen secured the perimeter and waited for the grain truck and the Chicken Handling and Tactics team, newly formed by the state police, to arrive and load up the perpetrators. The grain-scoop ploy had become standard police procedure by this time.

"Whew!" the Chief said, joining Smedley. "That was a close one."

"Yeah," Smedley answered. "Two points difference! I thought it might go into overtime."

"Not the game," the Chief said. "The chickens."

"Oh. Of course."

"Let's see your schematic there. I want to make sure I understand, in case this ever happens again."

Smedley gave the Chief the paper he'd been keeping notes on.

"That's great, Smedley. As long as you keep luring the chickens onto the carpet and off the court, the basketball players can run back and forth across the court. What a plan! What do you call it?"

Smedley thought for a moment.

"I think I'll call it a transistor," he said.

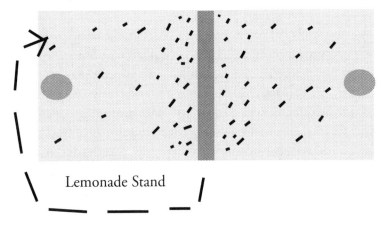

Lemonade Stand

Oscillators

The word "oscillate" means "to go back and forth in rhythm." Pendulums oscillate, the playground swing oscillates, a flag in a breeze oscillates. Many fun activities involve oscillation. Electrically, an oscillator is a device that causes current to pulse or alternate rhythmically.

Our spark-gap transmitter was a primitive sort of oscillator. We started with direct current, and we wound up with a spark of alternating current leaping between two contacts. We could not, however, control its frequency, and much current was wasted by resistance, reluctance, self-induction, and the creation of unwanted frequencies. There are better ways to get the job done.

Picture a transistor amplifier. The power circuit, or "output," is driving a speaker, and the input, or control circuit, includes a microphone. We snap our fingers, and a tiny fraction of a second later, we hear our "snap" amplified through the speaker. After repeating this game for perhaps a half-hour, it will become boring. To spice it up a bit, we move the microphone closer to the speaker. We snap our fingers. A fraction of a second later, we hear a much louder snap from the speaker. This time, the microphone also "hears" the speaker and feeds the sound back into the input circuit. We hear a third snap, which is the echo amplified. The microphone picks up this sound, and feeds it back to be amplified yet again. Our snap is repeated hundreds of times, automatically, and each one is an amplified version of the previous one. This is called "feedback." Part of the output of the amplifier is "fed back" and used as input. If you don't turn the thing off quickly it may get louder and louder until it destroys your speakers. If it is adjusted carefully (move the microphone away from the speaker until it is exactly the right distance), it will not get louder, but will just keep repeating itself forever.

With carefully adjusted feedback, and a little luck, your amplifier and speaker can maintain an ear-piercing shriek until the neighbors have you hauled away. The police may not care that all you did was snap your fingers once. They will not agree that it is wonderful you can feed output back into input and cause a self-sustaining chain reaction of snaps, so rapid that you can't distinguish them. They will give you a stern warning, and probably confiscate this book.

Neither of us want that.

We can enjoy a similar good time without risking jail by eliminating both the microphone and the speaker. Yes, ladies and gentlemen: silent feedback. We'll just run a wire from the output to the input. Since the input circuit is designed to handle little currents, we'll add a resistor to restrict the amount of feedback we get.

We turn on the switch. Our amplifier has no real "input." However, before the junctions can establish their charges, a tiny momentary flicker of current will flow. That's all we need. That little electronic finger snap is amplified, part of the amplified current is fed back to the input, where it is amplified, and we're in business. Our output current pulses on and off, with part of the current from each pulse providing the input for the next.

Since our device isn't attached to anything but itself, your friends may not be impressed. There is no way to tell if it's "working." If they try to jeer, you know what to do. Use jargon on them.

The speed of the pulses that we both know your oscillator is producing will be determined by your choice of transistors, resistors, and voltage. And, of course, by luck. If you want more control than that, add a filter.

There are many ways to design oscillators. They differ in their plans for returning feedback to the input circuit and in their plans for controlling frequency. Naturally, each and every variation has been given a name. They all do the same thing, in basically the same way: They cause electricity to alternate or pulse at some fairly specific frequency by using part of an amplifier's output as input.

The Old KaBoom

"KaBoom" was the registered trade name of a robot designed to shoot tennis balls across a net, so a player could practice returning serves without a partner. All you had to do was touch the machine's head and it would shoot five tennis balls, one after the other, one second apart.

The inventor was proud of his design, but the buying public soon discovered one serious flaw: You had to touch KaBoom before it would fire. If you touched it yourself, then raced back to your own side of the net, three or four practice balls would fly past while you were in transit, or even hit you in the back. Some people couldn't make it to their side of the net in time to return even one serve. People who tried to use KaBoom by themselves found it a valuable aid to aerobic conditioning, but not completely satisfactory for improving one's form. One alternative was to have a friend stand next to the machine and pat it on the head every now and then, but friends willing to spend that time would probably just as soon play some tennis with you.

KaBoom never got off the ground.

A few people, however, figured out that you could use KaBoom just fine if you treated it like an oscillator. The robot, they reasoned, was sort of an amplifier. On its maximum setting it could fire those tennis balls hard enough to kill a cow, yet a gentle pat on the head would control it: the amplifier principle. These enterprising players simply aimed their return shots at its head. As long as they could hit it once every five shots, they could practice all day long. These return shots were the equivalent of feedback in an oscillator.

As their aim improved, tennis players discovered another design oddity, one that made the old KaBoom seem even more similar to an oscillator, a flaw which eventually forced the manufacturer to recall and destroy all the machines. Each time a player managed to score a hit on the machine's head, it immediately began shooting a new series of five tennis balls, each a second apart, concurrently with the first five. It didn't wait to finish the first group. Perhaps you see the problem. If you managed to return the first ball and hit KaBoom on the head (say a half-second after it fired it toward you), it would immediately launch ball "one" of the second group; then, only a half-second later, it would shoot ball "two" of the first group. As a reward for his skill, a player was now attacked by a speeding tennis ball, not once a second, as he had planned, but once every half-second. Of course, the last thing he wanted at that point was to score another hit.

The final straw landed on KaBoom's back the day a Norwegian fellow living in Southern California set up the device at his home tennis court, without pausing to consider that his court was surrounded by a tall concrete wall. He turned on the robot and, remarkably, scored direct hits with his first three shots. To his horror, he realized that he would now be pummeled by at least a dozen balls in rapid succession. In panic, he began swinging wildly to fend off the fuzzy missiles. A particularly unlucky return struck the speed control lever, increasing it to near-fatal levels. At this increased velocity, each ball bounced off the concrete wall, back over the net, directly at KaBoom. Sheer luck dictated that a few of these automatic return shots would also hit the old KaBoom, ensuring a hellishly steady stream of Day-Glo projectiles hurtling over the net.

It was not a pretty sight. Alerted by his cries, neighbors ran to the poor Norwegian's aid, but were afraid to step onto the court because of the nightmare of tennis balls screaming from wall to wall. Only when the KaBoom finally ran out of balls were they able to help the whimpering, babbling, and badly bruised former tennis player from the court.

An oscillator, like the KaBoom, is an amplifier that feeds some of its output back into its control circuit, or input. Like the old KaBoom, it can develop very high frequencies. Like the KaBoom, once you get it set up right, it needs no pat on the head to keep it going.

Ice Ease

We've seen it a thousand times: some failed experiment leads to an important discovery. So it was when Isley Ease, the famous Norwegian photographer, decided to apply his skills to the building of electronic components. Wouldn't it be neat, he thought, if you could duplicate electronic circuits as cheaply and easily as you can reproduce photographs? The man was obviously a genius. Until this book was written, Mr. Ease ("Ice" to his friends) received no credit.

His thinking went like this: A resistor can be a very thin section of conductor. A thin wire has more resistance than a thick one. A piece of foil shaped like this:

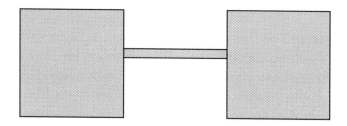

would act like a conductor. The thin section would act like a resistor. Two conductors close together but separated by an insulator, like this:

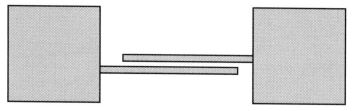

would act as a capacitor. It occurred to Mr. Ease that he could build many different components just by shaping conductors creatively. Aluminum foil or any other conductor, cut to precise shapes, could be used for resistors or capacitors. If he could make photographs of these shapes, he could duplicate them photographically. This would be cheap and convenient. He got excited. How about a coil, he thought? He came up with this two-dimensional coil:

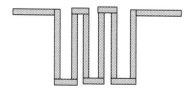

Then it occurred to him that he could make junction diodes and transistors by starting with very thin layers of P and N material joined together like wet sheets of paper and simply cutting away the excess. He knew that certain chemicals, when exposed to light and then processed, become impervious to acid. If he coated sheets of semiconducting material with these photoresistant chemicals, then used a photographic negative to control which sections were exposed to light, he could dip the whole works in acid and let it etch away everything but the shapes he had drawn to work as components.

So far, the man had a good idea. Where he faltered was in the application. He envisioned employing this technique to make huge circuits, the sized of a blackboard, to use as teaching aids. He thought he could simply draw these circuits on a piece of paper, then enlarge them onto slabs of silicon he had coated with photosensitive material. After developing these huge images of shapes that would act like resistors, capacitors, coils, transistors, and diodes, and dipping them in acid, he hoped to have a wall-sized design that would actually act as a working electrical circuit, yet be large enough for students in the back of the room to see.

The problem was that Ice used the wrong lens to make his enlargement. Rather than an enlarging lens, he accidentally used a reducing lens. When his process was finished, it worked beautifully. All the components worked as he had planned, but the whole circuit was about the size of a pin head. He was disgusted. His dream was shattered. He could see no use for a microscopic circuit. Although he had invented integrated circuits (Which are still sometimes referred to as "Ice Ease'), he didn't know it.

Before drifting into oblivion, he fed the original IC to his goldfish.

Didja-Didja-Didja-Didja Wanna Dance?

Paul Revere was one of the earliest popularizers of the "digital" concept. He said, "Okay buddy, have one light on for sure. That's how I'll know you're up in the church bell tower. Your other light will either be on or off. Let me see one light if the British soldiers are coming by land, two if they're coming by sea. And I on the opposite shore will be."

All digital equipment is based on his concept. Information can be translated into a code that boils down to: "Is the darn lantern on or off?" These days, instead of lanterns, we use switches. Information is "digitized" or encoded into a lengthy and elaborate pattern of "ons" and "offs." Once digitized, we can store the information (as we do in compact discs and computer disc drives), we can communicate with it (as we do with modems and FAX machines), and we can change, manipulate, compare, and process it (as we do with computers).

A pattern of "ons" and "offs" can be thought of as a series of "ones" and "zeros." When we make that mental leap, we open a whole new door. Digitized information is information converted into numbers, and is now subject to the many complicated operations of mathematics that men have been devising for centuries. Many people believe that the sky is now the limit. Everything can be digitized, and mathematics is supreme and infallible.

Unfortunately, I feel the same uneasiness about mathematics that I feel about electrons.

But that's another book. In fact, it's two books. If you share my uneasiness about math, you might enjoy a book I wrote with Jim Loats (a math professor) called *Algebra Unplugged*, or its exciting sequel, *Calculus for Cats*. If this seems like crass commercial self promotion to you, then you are very perceptive. If it irritates you, rather than merely apologize, let me suggest you read one of my novels, perhaps *The Land of Debris and the Home of Alfredo*. That should calm you right down. No need to thank me.

Early computers used little mechanical switches or cumbersome vacuum tubes. Later they used transistors. With the proper bias voltage, a transistor is a great switch. Two transistors tied together can act as a switch that will stay on or off, as long as power is available, until you change them. Perfect for storing a digital one or zero.

When integrated circuits were developed, which can have thousands of transistors on a speck of material too small to cause a sneeze, the world "went digital." Pocket calculators, digital watches, personal computers, modems, FAX machines, and compact-disc players became commonplace and inexpensive.

Armed with the simplest possible digital device, Paul Revere started the most powerful country the world has ever known.

Imagine what he could have done with a handful of ICs.

Reality Intrudes

Halloween night in Boulder is like Mardi Gras. Twenty thousand wildly costumed revelers crowd the streets, singing, dancing, and partying just as hard as they can figure out how to. You can tell it's a college town by the amount of brain power invested in unusual costumes. Against the dramatic background of the whispering Rocky Mountains, downtown Boulder becomes, for one night, an ocean of clowns, scarecrows, and witches. Man-sized insects prowl through the evening, walking cardboard noses sniff at pretty girls, human headlights blink on and off. Princesses and kings laugh and joke with six-foot eggs, while newspapers with heads watch from the shadows. Giant stalks of celery hold hands with computer terminals that have somehow grown legs.

My kind of town, I thought, as I stepped out the hotel door and into the moving human ocean. It was already dark and chilly. Except for the warmth of the crowd, my jacket would have been too light. I was wondering how I was supposed to find the Magician among all these people, when I noticed a very pretty girl dressed as a belly dancer walking beside me. She didn't seem to be cold, despite her flimsy costume. I decided that the Magician was better equipped to find me than I was to find him and let myself be swept away by the crowd.

Years ago, the main street of Boulder had been closed and replaced with trees and sidewalks. The crowd filled this mall completely for blocks and blocks. Every restaurant and bar along the way seemed to have some sort of entertainment. The smell of fresh garlic and oregano flowed from an Italian restaurant, along with the sound of a guitar and a man and woman singing. Sizzling steak and onion wafted from the door of another, to the strains of a country-western group. The aroma of cinnamon coffee and sweet pastries, and the sound of folk music came from another. I could hear a rock band in the distance.

Then I heard something weird and unworldly. A melodic, almost human, wailing sound, like a flute or an amplified violin, came from a small restaurant. This siren was somehow irresistible to me; I worked my way to the edge of the crowd and went in.

Fred's Steakhouse was a small cafe, clean, comfortable, and homey. The stage was barely big enough for the two men who sat there, playing the odd music. One of them was a tall and handsome blond, with incredibly blue eyes, playing guitar. The other man, also tall and angular, had black hair and a neat black beard. He could have been Abraham Lincoln. Between his knees he held a hand-saw, which he was bending with one hand while he stroked it with a violin bow: a musical saw. The two were intent on their music. I recognized the piece as a Bach bourree. Amazingly, it was excellent. The saw hit every note perfectly. The guitarist was perhaps the best I'd ever seen. Because of his concentration, he looked like one of those stiff, Germanic, perfectionist types with no sense of humor, but when the song ended, his face exploded into a bright smile, he nodded to the saw player and reached for his cup of coffee. Sometimes, I thought, things are not what they seem. The saw player laughed loudly, made a few bad saw puns, then they launched into *Take Five*.

"We've been waiting for you."

I whirled around. The Magician stood before me.

"There is little time. This way." I followed him to a table in the corner. Mike and Belinda were already drinking hot chocolate. The waitress brought one for me as I sat down. "I must set a trap for my enemies before they can set their own for me. A spell of the necessary strength will take some time. Luckily, Boulder is very disorienting to these men. But they are ruthless and cruel. If I fail, they will seek you out, just as I did. They will show you no mercy. I'm afraid your life is now at risk as well. Tell me about vacuum tubes. But be brief."

"Does the time-travel machine use tubes?" I asked incredulously. "Nobody uses tubes any more."

"It uses them."

I sensed the urgency in his voice and began. "A vacuum tube is a glass enclosure, like a light bulb. Most of the air has been pumped out of it, creating a vacuum. Electricity moves through a vacuum more easily than it does through air."

"Why don't they use plastic instead of glass?"

"I don't think anyone ever thought of it," I answered.

"Interesting. In the future they do. Continue."

"Right. A hot filament, or cathode, in the tube will be surrounded by a negative charge. Current can flow away from this negative charge to a metal plate, or anode, within the tube, but it can't flow from the plate back to the cathode. The charge repels it. So a vacuum tube diode is a one-way valve for electricity.

"If you put a screen, or grid, between the two elements, you have a triode. The charge on the grid will affect the flow of current. By varying that charge, you can use a small voltage to control a large current."

The Magician shook his head impatiently. "Fine, fine," he said. "That's not it. What about transistors."

I looked at him. His reply suggested that he was close to solving the problem with the time-travel machine. He had narrowed the possibilities and was waiting for me to fill in some bit of information. Some key fact...

He tapped his fingers on the table. I went on.

"Transistors and junction diodes are made of semiconducting materials like silicon. With one kind of impurity, a silicon crystal will tend to develop a positive charge (P-type). With a different impurity, it will tend to develop a negative charge (N-type). Where P-type material and N-type material touch each other, they create an interface called a "junction." The junction has a very thin section called the "depletion zone" which is a combination of the two types of material and is a poor conductor. On each side of this depletion zone, opposite charges will tend to build. Since electricity moves from negative toward positive, current will flow much more easily across a PN junction in the N to P direction. A diode is nothing more than a device with one of these junctions.

"This is interesting," I continued, warming to my task. "When the negative charge moves, they say that electrons are moving. When the positive charge moves, they say the "holes" are moving. They call positive charges "holes.""

"A transistor has two junctions arranged so that electricity can flow in neither direction through it. By adding a control circuit to drain the charges away, a tiny current can determine how much resistance a transistor will have to the main current. That's what a transistor is, really. A variable resistor. Transistors can be used as either little electronic switches or as amplifiers."

"That's not it either." The Magician was clearly nervous. He wanted to ask me a question, but hesitated. I think he was afraid he would give away some secret. Finally he decided to risk it.

"What's a fuse?" he asked.

"What?"

"A fuse. Like this." He held out his hand and showed me a small glass tube that had obviously gotten too hot. "I think this is my problem. What does it do?"

"Didn't I explain fuses to you?"

"I assumed we had not yet reached them."

"Actually they're pretty simple. Remember when we were talking about how some electricity is converted to heat whenever it goes through resistance?"

"That was some time ago."

"Right. Well, if enough current goes through a wire, it will get hot enough to melt it. Arc welders use this principle to melt pieces of metal together. We don't want any of our expensive components to melt if too much current accidentally goes through them, so we add a fuse. It's supposed to be the weakest link in a circuit. A fuse might be nothing more than a thin wire that will get hot enough to melt at some predictable current level. When it does, it breaks the circuit. If the current never goes above that level, the fuse won't melt. It will be just another resistor in a circuit."

"You mean I could just replace this with a wire?"

"Well, sure. Unless there's some reason too much current was flowing in the first place. Without the fuse to stop it, that extra current could damage some other component. Fuses are cheap. Whenever you replace a fuse, you just saved the cost of a more expensive component. A fuse you can reset is called a circuit breaker."

"A fuse could melt because of a power surge, though, couldn't it, even if the rest of the circuit was completely operational? Like if lightning struck nearby. If nothing else was damaged, in an emergency, I could just replace the fuse with a conductor."

"Did lightning strike near the time machine?"

"There was a certain amount of artificial lightning involved in my escape."

"You made lightning?"

"It was necessary."

"Well, yeah, that could have blown a fuse. This one is obviously fried."

"That's it, then. I will replace it. But first, I must set my trap."

"What kind of a trap will you set?"

The Magician smiled, a narrow-eyed smile that made me shiver.

"The futurist and his men have followed me to Boulder. They must not follow me farther, or return to their own time. Others that follow them must also be ensnared. I have already ensured that they will be drawn, like the insects that they are, to this time and this location. Now I will cast a spell upon the place that will keep them here. It must be a large and powerful spell, yet subtle, so that others do not notice…"

He stopped.

"There he is!"

We followed the Magician's gaze to a man standing in the doorway of the restaurant. Unlike the other revelers, he wore a black suit with a tasteful red tie. He was clean-shaven and his hair was neatly trimmed. He stood out like a clown at a funeral. He looked around the room, examining each table's occupants. I froze when his eyes stopped at our table. Amazingly, he didn't seem to recognize the Magician, and he finally turned and walked back out the door.

I looked at the Magician. His eyes were closed, his head was lifted toward the ceiling in concentration. So, I thought. That's why the futurist didn't see us. The Magician opened his eyes.

"There are several of them," he said. "Come quickly."

We followed him into the street, through the crowd, and to an old theater building, apparently long deserted, that was not far away. The door opened before us, as if by magic, and we followed the Magician down narrow wooden stairs into a maze of basement hallways and tiny storage rooms.

"This is the spot," he said, stopping in a tiny room. "I shall need exactly one hour to complete the spell. Once I begin, I will be vulnerable. They will detect my location, and I will be unable to defend myself. You must keep them from me for that hour."

Mike and I looked at each other, and then at Belinda.

"We'll do our best," I said.

"They will not be subtle," he said. "Guard the front door to the building." He stood very still, raised his face, and closed his eyes. Torches appeared on the floor in a circle around him, their flames dancing, casting weird, moving shadows on the walls. A quiet humming sound swelled around the old man, as if invisible druids had joined him and were chanting quietly to themselves. I thought I could smell incense. The Magician, deep in his trance, was oblivious to all.

"Let's boogie," said Mike, and we hurried up the labyrinth of stairways. I checked the time. Exactly 11 o'clock. It figures, I thought. His hour lasts until midnight.

By the time we got to the glass-and-metal front door, there were a dozen men in black business suits outside it, whispering to each other. As the Magician predicted, they had easily been able to locate us. Through the glass we could see them clearly in the light of the street lamps and moon. Because the inside of the theater was completely dark, we knew they could not see us. But that glass door would never keep them out. I wasn't even sure it was locked. They might only need to pull on the metal door handle.

"Allow me," Mike whispered. He tiptoed over to the door, put one hand on the metal and waited. After a moment, one of the futurists decided to try it. As soon as he touched the handle, sparks flew from it. He cursed and jumped back.

"It's electrified!" he shouted. By listening to their conversation we learned that they had two weapons back in their time-travel machine. Two men were sent to get them.

"Boy!" Mike whispered. "That felt good!" There were a few advantages to being on friendly terms with electricity. We all knew, however, that Mike had delayed them only for a few moments.

"I have an idea," I said. "If we can just distract these guys, keep them busy until the spell is complete... Can you help me get out there?"

Mike grinned and pointed at a street lamp. It began to glow brighter and brighter. The futurists, puzzled, turned away from the door to stare at it.

"Go, bro'," said Mike.

I walked out the door unnoticed and stood behind them.

"Excuse me," I said. Startled, they whirled around to face me. Now that I was close to them, I realized what hard, cruel faces they had. I was scared to death, but tried to act calm.

"I'd like to see your permit," I said.

"Our what?"

"Your full-moon permit. You do have one, don't you?"

They looked at each other. I was betting that government in the future was filled with nasty little regulations and obscure permits, and that these guys' worst fear was breaking some dumb little law they didn't even know about.

"Of course we have it," one of them said, lying with conviction. "But I don't think we have to show it to you. Perhaps you'd care to show us some identification."

I laughed.

"You boys aren't from around here, are you? That's not the procedure." I took a box of matches out of my pocket and waved it quickly at them. "There," I said. "They'll begin processing this video downtown. In case there are any problems." I spoke into the matchbox. "Just a routine check for a full-moon permit. I'm in front of the old theater. Next check in 10 minutes." It was the best I could think of at the moment. I wanted them to think that if they did something to me, someone would be looking for them.

210

I turned to the futurists who watched me in obvious confusion. "Now, which one of you has the permit?"

"He'll be back in a minute."

"Fine," I said. "I'll wait. What do you gentlemen think of the burnt-toast hoodwink phenomena?" They looked at each other. Their studies of this time period had been very thorough, but like most people, they were unprepared for the loud and confident use of meaningless jargon.

"I'm not sure," one of them said, obviously thinking quickly. "I go back and forth. What do you think?"

"Oh, I'm for it," I said. "I don't think it will ever replace the wishbone, of course, but if your fast-break isn't working, what choice do you have? I suppose you could go to the bump-and-run, or even the flea-flicker, but you'll never get a seventh inning stretch out of it. No, I think you have to clarify your onions, put the pedal to the metal, and back-flush your radiator. Don't you agree?"

They all nodded vigorously in agreement. Out of the corner of my eye I could see the other two approaching with the weapons. I looked at my watch. Eleven thirty.

"Listen, if your friend isn't here soon with that full-moon permit, I'm going to have to ask you to bring it to the office tomorrow. Will you do that for me?"

They promised that they would. I saw them motion to their friends to wait. They didn't want to draw any more attention to themselves than they had to. I talked aimlessly for as long as I could, until I saw their patience wearing thin, then I left them, walked down the sidewalk, and watched them from the crowd. Now what could we do? The men pointed one of their gun-like weapons at the door. Silently, the door simply vaporized. It just disappeared. My heart sank. There was nothing we could do to stand up to weapons like that. We had lost.

But the futurists didn't go through the door immediately. They seemed agitated. I shook my head. Something didn't look right to me either. Then I understood. The futurists' skin was beginning to glow red. So was mine and everyone else's in the costumed mob. The futurists stopped in their tracks. The wire leading to the street lamp seemed to swell up like a fat gray snake, and a flickering fog of many colors settled over the delighted Halloween crowd. Visible radio waves, I guessed. Mike had done it again.

The fog was so dense and distracting that no one could see more than a foot in front of them. The crowd thought it was some special effect provided by the city for their party. One fellow behind me thought he was back in the 1960s and stoned out of his mind. He sounded nostalgic. I was sure that the futurists were stymied and confused, but I didn't know how long Mike could keep it up. It took a lot of his energy to do this little trick. I held my watch close to my face. Ten 'till. Hang in there, Mike, I thought.

But the fog was already clearing, my skin was glowing less brightly, the magnetism surrounding the wires faded. I saw Mike stumble out the door of the theater and fall weakly to the sidewalk. I started running toward him, although I had no idea how I'd be able to help. Two futurists had "guns." One pointed his at Mike. Even exhausted, Mike moved too quickly for him, rolling out of the way at the last second. The weapon vaporized a huge section of cement where Mike had been an instant earlier. The man cursed and aimed again.

"Let's do some inductance," Mike said faintly, pointing his finger at the weapon. I guessed he was producing electromagnetic waves somehow, inducing eddy currents in the weapon. Sure enough, the weapon began to glow red-hot from its own resistance to these currents. The man dropped it in sudden pain and surprise. "Just like Star Trek," Mike said.

The other armed futurist was already aiming at Mike. Once again, at the last possible instant, my green friend rolled away and another slab of concrete disappeared. But this time, Mike had misjudged a bit. His motion carried him too far, and his head slammed into the brick building. His eyes closed, his body relaxed, and he lay motionless on the cement.

"Mike!" I yelled, still running toward the group. The futurist smiled wickedly and pointed his gun at the prone and helpless

Greenie. I was still too faraway. "Mike!" I yelled again, knowing there was nothing I could do to save him.

"Lights out, sucker!" the man said, taking careful, deliberate aim.

But he didn't get a chance to pull the trigger. A figure leaped from the theater doorway and moved toward them so quickly the futurist had no chance to react. This human blur was upon him within a heartbeat, kicking the weapon from his hand, jamming an elbow into his belly, then grabbing his arm and head and skillfully throwing him to the ground.

It was Belinda.

The others closed in around her. By now I too had reached them. I swung my fist and connected with the surprised face of the closest one. I saw blood begin to trickle from his nose, just before I felt his own fist hit my stomach like a sledge-hammer.

That's it for me, I thought, as pain and nausea filled my body. I tried to inhale, but could not. I couldn't make a sound. I realized I could not even keep my balance. Clutching my stomach I fell to the ground and watched helplessly.

Despite the fact that she was still dressed in her flowing medieval gown, and despite the fact that she was outnumbered eleven to one, Belinda attacked the futurists in business suits as if she were a Ninja warrior. One by one they fell before her onslaught of flying fists and leaping kicks. The sidewalk became quickly littered with their groaning forms. They tried to surround her, they tried to grab her arms. Each time she met them with a precise and effective counter move. They came at her in groups, they came at her individually. The results were the same. They felt her fist crush into their chests, her elbow or knee crack their ribs, her foot smash against their chins. These evil men of the future were clearly out-manned by the beautiful medieval tigress, this lovely and elegant fighting machine. Then I realized what her role had been with the Magician. She was not his assistant. She was his bodyguard.

Finally only one man was standing. Belinda turned, half crouching, to face him, then stopped. Somehow he had found the weapon, and he aimed it directly at her.

"This will be a shame," he said, and his voice was cruel. "I would like to take you with me to the future. Perhaps, with the right restraints, you could prove entertaining. But I'm afraid that would be too dangerous. There is no room for strong women in my world."

I looked at my watch. Two minutes until midnight—we'd come so close! I still couldn't move or speak. Mike was breathing, but he remained unconscious. All of Belinda's fighting skills were useless against a weapon like the one the man held. She held herself very straight, prepared to die with dignity and pride, like the warrior she was.

"Good-bye, my dear," he said, raising the gun. I saw his finger begin to move. I closed my eyes. There was a loud thunking sound, like a pillow thrown against a wall. I wanted to cry.

"What the...!" The futurist sounded startled and confused.

I opened my eyes again. Something had hit him in the face just before he pulled the trigger, and he had flinched. Belinda still stood before him, looking as surprised as he did. He spit a feather out of his mouth and looked around. Then it came at him again, something flying through the air, attacking from above, like a little dive bomber. He ducked, the thing flew past, then turned to circle back. I felt a lump growing in my throat, as I began to understand.

It was a duck, wearing a little red bandanna around its head, pride and determination shining from his eyes and feathers. At last I could speak.

"Bruce!" I shouted. He dipped a wing in acknowledgement, then dived again. This time a whole squadron followed him, slamming into the wide-eyed futurist like little kamikaze pilots. The man tried to fend them off with his arms, but it was no use. He fell to his knees, sneezing uncontrollably, and Belinda calmly took the weapon from his hand.

"It is done!"

Everyone turned to the Magician who had appeared in the doorway. He looked supremely confident, and I knew we had won. He pointed a bony finger at the weapon Belinda held. It vanished. "We don't need any of those lying around," he said.

He waved casually in Mike's direction. Mike's eyes opened.

"You rang?" Mike said, sitting up and rubbing his head. The Magician nodded in the direction of Bruce, who was still circling above us. The valiant bird dipped his left wing and careened off into the night, his troops following behind him.

The futurists began to get up off the ground. Something was different about them. They no longer looked dangerous, but I was not sure why. It was not simply defeat I saw in their faces, but dazed confusion. They were no longer interested in the Magician, and didn't even look in his direction. They seemed to have forgotten him, forgotten the recent battle, forgotten both the past and the future. I heard one mumbling something that sounded like poetry as he shuffled around. They seemed helpless, disorganized, and somewhat pathetic as they wandered off and were quickly absorbed by the Halloween crowd.

Some spell, I thought to myself.

"We leave at noon tomorrow," the Magician said.

Epilog

The Magician stood shoulder-high in a big wooden barrel: It was the time travel machine. The scientists of the future had designed it to be inconspicuous in any era.

"I don't know that I understand what electricity *is* yet," he said. "You've talked about electrons and Greenies and buffalo and ducks. A lot of it still seems confusing to me. But I would no longer be afraid to study it. Anyway, we did fix the machine. Perhaps some day I will return and we can discuss it in more detail."

"You bet," I said, but I had already decided that my next book would be a novel. Writing nonfiction is just too dangerous. The Magician smiled thinly, as if reading my mind.

"Perhaps science is a little like magic, after all," he said. "People will claim to understand the magical things in the world, like music and happiness, but in the end, we each make up our own definitions. If we study them too closely, the magic disappears. And we can never understand them perfectly, anyway. Perhaps electricity is like that."

"Don't say that to a science teacher."

"They won't invent science teachers until centuries after I'm dead," he said. He turned to Mike. "Are you ready?" Mike and I shook hands. We had gone fishing one last time that morning and said all our good-byes.

"Later, bro'," he said, then he vanished. The Magician had transported him back to Utah, to the spot by the lake he had come from, so that he could return home.

"Belinda has decided to stay in this place," the Magician said. "You may see her again. She has gotten a job teaching some skill, I forget the name."

"Assertiveness," I reminded him. Something was still bothering me. "By the way," I said, trying to sound casual, "what kind of spell did you cast on Boulder? Those guys sure seemed confused!"

"The most powerful of all," he said. "And the most difficult to break. I cast the spell of Love. If others from the future try to follow me to Boulder, they will not be able to keep from falling in love. Men in love are helpless puppies. Completely useless as soldiers. I am safe."

He turned on the machine, it began to make a low rumbling sound. He had to speak loudly to be heard above it.

"I granted Belinda her wish of changing the century of her life, as well as giving her a new wardrobe. I transported Mike to Utah, and helped recharge him with a few small bolts of lightning. Is there some small parting favor I can grant to you?"

I swallowed hard, screwed up my courage, and asked for a big one.

"Season tickets to the Denver Broncos?"

He shook his head. The barrel began to vibrate and chatter violently. I could smell ozone and cinnamon.

"I'm good, Kenn," he said. "But not that good. How about this. You enjoy puzzles. I have hidden 10,000 dollars somewhere in the United States. If you think about it, you know where it is. Good luck."

"What?" I shouted, but he didn't respond. He simply waved his hand, then closed his eyes. "What?" I screamed.

The sound became louder, dust rose in a cloud from the floor. The barrel began to glow a brilliant white. Further conversation was impossible. The old man nodded in my direction. The dirt in the air and the increasingly intense light hurt my eyes, but I wanted to see how the thing worked. I began to cough.

Just before I had to close my eyes, I saw the barrel rise a foot or two off the ground and begin to spin slowly, 'round and 'round and 'round.

What other readers have said about this book:

"This is a totally painless way to learn about something that affects our lives every day. If only we could get Amdahl to write books on history, geography, grammar, math, and brain surgery, we'd have no need for schools."
Big Books from Small Presses

"Here at last is a book that explains electricity in terms simple enough even for the 'scientifically impaired.' Though uncredentialed and unconventional— professing disbelief in the existence of electrons even as he describes their behavior— Amdahl is nevertheless wise, witty, and very effective, aiding comprehension of abstruse jargon and arcane concepts with gimmicks like dancing chickens, wizards, and green buffalo."
A Common Reader

"...rinfrescanti, divertenti e incredibilmente semplici che, come in un romanzo di fanatascienza, introducono il lettore "ingenuo" nel mondo della elettricita, ne spiegano con chiarezza ed efficacia tutti i persunti "misteri" e, passo dopo passo, lo portano sui piu alti sentieri della fisica elementara, disperdendo, una volta giunti in cima alle..."
L 'Arena di Pola

"Most of all, the book is a thought-provoker and teacher, leading the reader with no background in science or math gently down the road to electrical enlightenment. It would be a useful supplement to any beginning course in electronics."
Old Colony Sound Lab

"Every millennium or so, a radical non-conformist type appears on the scene to challenge the status quo of science. In this case, the heretic postures that electronics doesn't have to be so difficult. Kenn Amdahl is to electronics manuals what Dr. Seuss is to children's books."
Scott Rundle, *B&W's Coda*

"Get ready to have a great time! This is an amazing book, packed with electronic concepts, off the wall analogies and "Little Greenies." Refreshingly non-technical, this is the book everyone is talking about."
Gateway Electronics

"Describing how series and parallel resistances work by comparing them to vehicles crossing bridges is a brilliant metaphor. Don't let non-ham friends or family members find this book in your library, though; if they read it, they'll find out that there's no big mystery to electronics and spoil your image of you as a master of a stupefying technical art."
Brian Battles, QST Magazine

"When someone suggested that I review [this book] I thought I was hitting a prema-
ture journalistic bottom. To my surprise, I learned an amazing amount rethinking
what I already knew, things that I had learned the hard way... At the end, the reader
"owns" these electrical concepts. More importantly, a person in possession of the
author's conception will find the world more exciting and magical."

Herb Reichert, *Sound Practices*

"This refreshing book is an excellent resource for teaching newcomers the basics of
electronics within a very non-technical framework."

Engineering Update, **National Public Radio**

"The problem with many books on electronics is that they are written by people who,
for some strange reason, feel you need to suffer. After reading *There Are No Electrons,*
I realized that it doesn't have to be that way. For those who are open minded, this book
is perfect. For those who believe that the study of electronics has to be a painful experience, let them stick to the textbooks. I'll take Bruce the duck and the break-dancing
chickens any day!" **Michele Guido,** *Installation News*

"Perhaps the best electronics book ever. If you'd like to learn about basic electronics
but haven't been able to pull it off, get *There Are No Electrons.* Just trust us. Get the
book *Monitoring Times*

"It's a fine, clever book and it deserves a wide readership." **Robert M. Hazen,**
Carnegie Institution of Washington,
co-author of *Science Matters: Achieving Scientific Literacy*

"Here is a book to be read for fun!" *Backwoods Solar*

"Amdahl's book has a serious purpose behind the flippancy and silliness: to teach
electricity and electronics to mathematics and physics anxiety sufferers."

Choice, **The American Library Association**

"If you're faint of heart, don't read this book. It may cause you to change! You may find
yourself understanding electronics in as clear a manner as you have ever understood
anything in your life. What a joy, after years of wanting to understand jargon like
'capacitive reactance,' that someone has finally figured out how to make this mind
understand." **Michael A. Tolfa,**
National Science Teachers Association

"If you're a little shaky on some of the basic concepts of electricity, check out this book by a wild man named Kenn Amdahl. This book is fun. I guarantee it's easier going than any textbook you've ever tried to read."

Car Audio and Electronics

"An entertaining and practical approach to learning the elementary physics of electricity."

Science News

"Indeed a unique approach to helping people understand how those pesky little electrons seem to work."

Dr. Wayne Green, publisher, 73 Amateur Radio Today

"Seeking a dry, straightforward electronics guide? Look elsewhere: there are plenty of books around. Having problems understanding electronics? Choose Amdahl's presentation, which rambles somewhat, but which offers a lively, unusual lesson on the elementary principles of electricity. Poetic comparisons and analogies of electronics to everyday life will penetrate the brains of those who typically have problems visualizing and understanding such an abstract subject. The result is both entertaining and educational."

The Bookwatch

"A bizarre cross between *Grimm's Fairy Tales* and Richard Brautigan's *Trout Fishing in America*... If any of you have ever tried to explain electricity to spouses, children, friends, or parents, only to see their eyes glaze over after a minute or two, this book could do the trick... Somehow, between the laughs, a real understanding of electricity unobtrusively takes hold."

Radio Electonics Magazine

"This piece of work probably will go farther to draw people into electronics than anything ever written."

Emil Venere

"I have already found *There Are No Electrons* to be useful to me in my hobby, ham radio. The practical and yet lively manner of presentation immediately caught my interest and held my attention throughout. I liked the understated sense of humor and imagery as presented through 'Greenies.' As an educator, I feel that the use of substitute imagery is a good learning device and helps take the mystery out of a seemingly complex area of study. A fine job of writing. It deserves to be read widely."

Dr. Roger Young, Director,
Center for Independent Study, University of Missouri

"Opening this book is like falling down a scientific rabbit-hole, an adventure in itself. Your perspective on electronics is turned upside down, you gain insights in the most bizarre ways. and you'll probably find that they stay with you for a good long time... The inspired, informative silliness makes the book a pleasure to read. Thank you, Mr. Amdahl, thank you. **West Coast Review of Books**

"The book is laced with sarcasm and irony, which have no real place in a text for novices, who cannot easily tell fact from fiction... the book should only be used by a teaching professional, who can safely extract the excellent images available for some situations and ignore the trash... it cannot be recommended."
Robert H. Cordella, Jr.
Office of Research and Development, CIA, Washington, D.C.

"*There Are No Electrons* has become required reading for all my coop students at Dow.
Bob Mostafapour,
Central Research, Dow Chemical Company

"Like a lighthearted melding of Mr. Wizard and the folks of National Lampoon, *There Are No Electrons* takes a radically different approach to electronics. Electrons are little green men on their way to a killer party; capacitors are parking lot sized traffic jams; Greenies, it seems, like to surf on magnetic flux. And why not? Even the experts must speculate the details of electron theory. Amdahl just sees things a little differently. You will too."
Videomaker Magazine

"The Mysteries of Electricity are Revealed in this bizarre and often amusing textbook-in-a-clown suit. It'll seem needlessly frivolous and even flippant to the annoying minority that have no trouble copping an A in physics. For the other four billion or so earth citizens, it's about the easiest and clearest course in basic electronics imaginable. It serves well as a refresher course or a solid introduction to the complicated stuff. The presentation is accessible to a sixth-grader, yet I'd guess that most adults would not be gagged by the author's antics. If you can hack this style of teaching, you'll get what you need."
The Whole Earth Review

"This book deserves to have songs written about it."
Michael Richards, on Amazon .com